Endorsements

"Highly descriptive testimonies of Servant Leadership! Through her personal experiences, Marcia Armstead reveals what it takes to be a successful and effective servant leader: a close relationship with God."

Roger M. Lindo, MA,
Religion/Andrews University

"In the broad mix of Christian literature there are instructive devotionals, confessional autobiographies and heart-warming mission stories. Marcia Armstead's, *A Journey in Servant Leadership*, combines them all! No pious proclamations, no lengthy formulas, no "my way or the highway" attitude, rather a daring and devoted life richly used by the hand of God. I found it hard to put down and you will too!"

Calvin B. Rock, Ph.D.

A Journey in Servant Leadership

Marcia B. Armstead

TEACH Services, Inc.
P U B L I S H I N G
www.TEACHServices.com • (800) 367-1844

Copyright © 2021 Marcia B. Armstead
Copyright © 2021 TEACH Services, Inc.
ISBN-13: 978-1-4796-1407-3 (Paperback)
ISBN-13: 978-1-4796-1408-0 (ePub)
Library of Congress Control Number: 2021916030

All Scripture quotations, unless otherwise noted, are taken from the KING JAMES VERSION (KJV), public domain.

Published by

TEACH Services, Inc.
P U B L I S H I N G
www.TEACHServices.com ● (800) 367-1844

Dedication

This book is dedicated to all my private and public supporters, my mentors, and those who have held me accountable for any and all missteps—facilitating my transformation into a more graceful and compassionate human being.

Preface

It has been two decades since Marcia B. Armstead wrote her first book, *The Complete Wo/Man: An Index to the Heart*[1] (published in 2002) and ten years since her second book, *Fragrance of God's Love: An Autobiography through the Love of My Friends,*[2] (published in 2010).

This book, *A Journey in Servant Leadership*, highlights some historical experiences but focuses primarily on the past decade of Marcia's life (2009–2019)—ten years of undeniable, God-directed servant-leadership experiences as the Assistant for Pastoral Care at the Colorado Springs Central SDA Church. As the author journeys through a series of challenges, opportunities, and assignments, you will truly understand that "God doesn't call the qualified, He qualifies the called,"[3] a beautiful thought based on 1 Corinthians 1:27–29.

Marcia's self-revealed ambitions, obligations, and deficiencies are presented as a travel log of experiences that led to an amazing lay ministry. You will learn how the hand of God guided the events of the last decade, in which she started as a volunteer and then became a pastoral staff member.

Under God's guidance, she developed her life skill of writing, and a passion for ministry. This partnership of writing and doing is the reason she has blessed so many through seminars, television programs, consulting, and nonfictional books.

Table of Contents

Preface. vii

Chapter 1   Earlier Years 11

Chapter 2   Retirement Aspirations. 20

Chapter 3   Never Say Never 26

Chapter 4   First, a Volunteer. 33

Chapter 5   Chosen, Qualified, Valued 50

Chapter 6   Listening to God 71

Chapter 7   Mentors and Friends. 82

Chapter 8   Hard to Walk Away 91

Chapter 9   What's Next 94

Chapter 10   Things I Have Learned. 96

Bibliography 98

Chapter 1

Earlier Years

B efore walking through the decennary period of my life, which was my last decade in local church ministry [2009–2019], I must first do some self-reflection and relate a few incredible things that happened to me between the years 1999 to 2009—events not mentioned in my earlier books. This first chapter deals with these noteworthy occurrences during those earlier years.

Have you ever wanted to climb to the top of a tree for a better view—to see a nearby mountain, a faraway waterfall, or a majestic image? And then, you realize this feat would be impossible without a ladder or without shoulders you could stand on or without some way to be hoisted inch by inch until you reached a comfortable vantage point. That was my mindset when I first arrived in Colorado Springs in 1999, as I stood in a valley trying to imagine what my future would be like. I knew where the ladder was. It was in the church; however, I had no notion or understanding of where, or if, shoulders would be available to me. Of course, I knew God definitely had a plan, and I needed to wait on Him.

My ladder was my first church in Colorado Springs, the Palace of Peace SDA Church, where I spent the first ten years volunteering as a church leader in Family Life and Singles Ministries, and one year as a Sabbath School superintendent. During these first ten years, I was also heavily involved in the community—as a volunteer chaplain at Memorial Hospital, as a seminar consultant, as the host of a radio and TV program—all while working full time for the Fourth Judicial District (courthouse) in Colorado Springs and attending college at night. Looking back at this time, I realize that God, and God alone, was my Provider, my Strength, and my Companion. While these years were tough, everything that I was doing for the Lord seemed effortless.

When I became a member of Palace of Peace Church in 1999, our pastor then was Bryan Mann and his beautiful wife was Valoree. As previously stated, it was here that I became involved in volunteer ministry activities and where I was happy to serve my church. As the widow of a pastor, I had never served actively as a department leader in any of the churches my late husband had pastored. So, with no church leadership desire or experience, I was new to hands-on involvement in church work, and I had never even attended a church board meeting. So, becoming involved at Palace of Peace was new for me, but I embraced it enthusiastically.

Valoree Mann was a soft-spoken and caring pastor's wife. She recommended The Complete Woman/Man Seminars consultants to present for a church group of another denomination. This was our first seminar in Colorado—a women's weekend held at the Quaker Ridge Conference Center in Woodland Park, Colorado. It was there that I met Christians from other faiths and one of my now life-long friends.

Pastor Mann was a great shepherding leader. I will share only one of the many kindnesses he did for our family. During the time he pastored us at Palace of Peace, one divine intervention stands out for me. It was an evening in which I was late for our weekly Prayer Meeting, and I wanted to be early in order to ask the pastor before the meeting to pray for my family. As I rushed into the foyer area of the church building, Pastor Mann was on his knees praying for the church, and, as I stood outside the door, I heard the pastor praying for me (a single mom, and a widow), and then he prayed for my children, calling each by name! As I listened to his intercession for us, I realized that he had asked God for exactly what we needed, and God answered his prayer!

It was a joy to know that I was part of a church family that not only loved its people, but also showed compassion when needed.

So, it was sooner, and not later, that I wanted to contribute to the work of the Lord as a volunteer in whatever area I was needed and wherever I was qualified to serve. It was while preparing to write this book that I came across some printed programs and church bulletins and realized how much volunteer work I had actually done while at Palace of Peace—serving as a department leader and then later as an elder.

Now, becoming the first female elder at the church was nothing more than a God-ordained assignment that prepared me for what was to come during the next decade. It was in the year 2006 that God showed me, in a dream, that there would soon be a female elder assigned to our church. Wow! Was I ever surprised! Not that I thought this could not happen—as I knew God well enough to understand that whatever He said would come to pass—but I wondered who that person would be. *Certainly, it would not be me*, I thought. Why? Well, being from the "old school," I honestly believed women should not occupy top-leadership roles in any church. Of course, I had spoken in many pulpits when I was invited to preach and/or do a seminar. And I thought this was acceptable, since I was just speaking for an hour or two, and this was not a permanent assignment. As I pondered this new possibility, I was confident that this revelation of eldership was not meant for me, and I thought, *But God, let me help you by recommending someone who I think could do the job.* As I contemplated which woman in the church might well fit this role, one individual stood out in my mind. I felt (for sure) God would place her in that position. So, I did not give this dream a second thought.

Time passed, and I had forgotten all about this dream. It was now four months later, and our nominating committee was meeting to select new church officers. That Tuesday evening, while on my way to the church for prayer meeting, my cell phone chimed. It was our new pastor, Michael Bruce Kelly, III. He said, "Sister Armstead, we are in a nominating committee meeting and your name has come up to serve as an elder in the church, would you be willing to accept this task?" Before he fully completed the question, the dream I had had returned to my memory, and the Holy

Spirit prompted me, *Say yes!* I could tell the pastor was somewhat surprised when I responded, "Sure Pastor, I will accept the nomination." Pastor Kelly knew enough about my ideology and was prepared to give a convincing argument as to why I should accept, but there was no need!

Well, here I was now an elder of the church—a novice, working with other experienced *male* elders. Before embracing all the ecclesiastical tasks that I imagine would be within the purview of eldership, Pastor Kelly and I sat together in his office, going over some of the responsibilities that it was my privilege to assume. He stated his belief that I had been *called* and was qualified for this position, and that he was confident in my abilities.

> *During one of our foot-washing, communion services, Pastor Kelly washed the feet of all his elders, including mine.*

Though I do not remember everything that we discussed in that meeting, one conclusionary advice has stuck with me until this day. The Pastor said, "Elder Armstead, please know that members are going to gossip, and they will approach you with rumors—but it is important as an elder that the gossip stops with you." What I believe he meant was this: You must either use your spiritual intellect to stop hearsay in its tracks or find a way to the root of the rumor and uproot it in a gentle, kind, and spiritual way. It seemed this was all that I needed to remember because I felt God had indeed called me to this position in which trustworthiness was of great importance.

Pastor Kelly, a much younger man than I, taught me, by example and engagement, how to truly serve in the capacity of an elder. He did one amazing act that I had never experienced before, or since, during his tenure at the church. It was during one of our foot-washing, communion services in which he washed the feet of all his elders. There are no adequate words to express now, or ever, what that action meant for me. All I can say is, it genuinely reminded me of how the disciples must have felt when Jesus washed their feet at the Last Supper. I will never forget, or truly be able to express, the feeling and life-changing impact this gesture had for me.

A couple of years later, I was ordained under the leadership of Pastor Melvin Warfield, Jr., Pastor Kelly's successor. Let me say that this ordination (to me) was not as spectacular an occurrence as others have portrayed a laying on of hands to be. I did not feel a great spiritual unction over me, as I had been led to believe, but this was not surprising. Why? Because God had already appointed and ordained me, so this ceremony was only an acknowledgment of His will, a confirmation of my acceptance to do His will, and an occasion witnessed by the church at large.

In hindsight, I know God had given me this position in preparation for something else, but I had not a clue that Our Father was preparing me to do ministry elsewhere. I was settled, content, and had no plans of saying adieu to Palace of Peace. But God had a plan! It was at this epilogue of my first ten years in Colorado that, in a vision, God showed me that I would be leaving Palace of Peace to minister at another church.

Farewell to Palace of Peace

God called me away from my activities at one congregation, but not from my friendships with many brothers and sisters in Christ. There were some in particular who were always a source of support and encouragement to me, and I will say just a little about those few. Sandra and Roy Morgan supported The Complete Woman/Man Seminars in the city of Colorado Springs—both financially and spiritually. Elder Roy Morgan was always a consoler and a spiritual counselor. These two individuals were not common people, but were always for the common good of the people based on biblical teachings. Sandra has never forgotten to send me a card for each of my birthdays ever since knowing her, and Roy has never met a stranger. His motto is this: we are all one in the eyes of God.

Vinnette and James Pope were, and are, also great supporters. When my first book was written, Vinnette sold most of the books in our local inventory, and I was encouraged by her to organize a book signing in Colorado Springs that was a highly successful event. Her husband, Elder James Pope, supported her in every endeavor to help us with book sales. When I first met them, he wanted to make sure I was saying and spelling his wife's name correctly. I still laugh when remembering how he would pronounce, spell, and then reiterate, "Two n's and two t's in Vinnette!" Even though this was appreciated, I would always laugh. And I still do when I reflect on those times and conversations. Like me, this couple was very particular and cognizant of misspellings—especially when it had to do with someone's name. That was admirable!

Rita and Ed Shuman were also supportive of our local seminars and are one of the most hospitable couples I have ever met. Friends, Sandra and Lee Jones, allowed me into their home whenever I needed to have a relaxing massage, as Lee [1940–2020] was a masseur—and he was the first in that profession who ministered to me. Usually, after a massage session, I would say, "I wish I could stay on this table and just go to sleep." He would respond, "You do not have to go home, but you sure can't stay here!" Sandra and I would always laugh about that. God allowed these two people into my life, and I so miss being his client.

Many, many more helped me in climbing my ladder. Worth mentioning are those who assisted (without charge) in The Complete Woman/Man Seminars and outreach in the city of Colorado Springs. Several volunteers from Palace of Peace would be featured as soloists and in groups. These individuals were singers Nickole Wilson-Semakula, Ayana Samuel, Morla Colby, Tia Kelly, and Lucius Davis. Also, Ruth McConnaughhay, Sylvia Williams (and all in the Williams family), Sandy and Carl Burks, and Angela Davis. Many others, even outside of our church, were exceptional co-servants and friends.

One amazing friend is Carletta Dickerson. A wonderful woman with a soft heart, who was very forthcoming, direct, and personable. (We grew close because I share some of those characteristics with her). Carletta, however, knows how to sing and direct musical groups. This is not my forte. She and I are close in age; and, although we may not talk or see each other often, our friendship is unalterable.

One of the most unforgettable things I remember her doing for me happened when my son, Jonathan, died. Carletta called when she heard the news and asked if there was anything she could do. I said, "No. Not right now. I'm going this afternoon to make funeral arrangements and will get back with you." She then asked if she could attend that meeting with me, as she lived not far from the funeral home. My response was, "No. I can handle this. Don't forget that I know the funeral home people because I have been there before helping several families with funeral arrangements; I'm a chaplain; and this will be easy for me." That afternoon, as the meeting began, a sudden feeling of deep sorrow and aloneness came over me. I could hardly speak and wished there had been someone there with me—just anyone. About a minute later, as I looked toward the door, Carletta was ushered into the meeting room. She sat with me and said little, but her presence was all I needed. Carletta also took a load off my shoulders when she volunteered to coordinate the service. This was something that came easily for her, and this allowed for a smooth memorial.

I love this woman and her family dearly, and I have beautiful memories of her mother, Gloria Bolden [1926–2012] who took me aside once or twice, after listening to my sermons and gave me constructive assessments. I loved Sister Bolden's honesty and her biblical knowledge, which she was always so willing to share—not just with me but with all who were willing to receive instruction and improve their public speaking.

Elder Sonia Johnson, an unquestionable woman of God, was my successor after I relinquished my eldership role at Palace of Peace in 2009. Before meeting Sonia, I first met her husband, Alton Johnson [1953–2007]. He had relocated to Colorado Springs (along with their son) before Sonia arrived. In meeting Alton, I observed his impeccable character traits. I knew he had to be married to a very extraordinary woman, whom he said would be arriving within a few months. When Sonia did come—and from the moment I saw this woman walking into the sanctuary—I knew this had to be Alton's wife. What was so amazing about this observation is that she walked in alone, and I had not

seen a picture of Sonia, neither did I know that she had even
been in town, but I instinctively knew who she was. In all my life,
this has never happened before or since. At present, Sonia serves
as the second female elder at Palace of Peace. How wonderful
is that! Our God always has a
replacement when He creates a
vacancy.

> *Every journey has a beginning, a purpose, and a destination and, with each step, we move closer and closer to God's ideal for our lives.*

The list of associates, mentors, and friends is not complete without mentioning Elder James and Minnie Rowe. They are the pillars and founders of Palace of Peace Church, even though their "birth church" was Colorado Springs Central. As pillars, they did what all good leaders do: they nurtured the flock, managed care of the physical plant, supported the pastors, housed and entertained guests in their home, and transported whoever needed their services.

This is the church family I left, but I still see and associate with them often. And, as I reflect on the pastoral leadership and care I was privileged to receive from our former pastors— Bryan Mann, Michael Kelly, and Melvin Warfield—I realize that I am a beneficiary of their faith in God, their prayers for me and family, and their ingenuity.

Each journey has a beginning, a purpose, and a destination. Certainly, no one arrives at the top of any mountain without starting the climb at a basepoint. My journey has been one of continual blessings. Yes, it has involved slipping and falling, getting up, resuming the climb, but always following the trajectory of purpose. Hope, faith, and longevity can be enormously propelling. And, with each step, as we move closer and closer to God's ideal for our lives; we will move upward through special encounters, personal relationships, and resolute achievements.

This epilogue of my time at Palace of Peace in 2009 was not the end of local church ministry, as I had hoped. In November of that year, I joined the Colorado Springs Central Church, and—contrary to *my* plans, which were to retire from the Fourth

Judicial District Courthouse; graduate from Colorado Christian University; write another book; travel; and relax—*God* had other plans in mind.

He allowed me to accomplish my aspirations and goals, and He also anointed me to minister at Central for another ten years.

Chapter 2

Retirement Aspirations

The year 2009–2010 was a pivotal time for me to ascertain what I wanted my sexagenarian years to resemble. I was heading into retirement and a life of ease. It was never my thinking, desire, or intention to do any type of mandatory work after my retirement in June 2010. I wanted to relax at home, travel, write more letters and books, reunite with friends I had not seen in years, and eventually settle in the state of Alabama (or Florida) where the majority of my friends lived and where the climate was warmer. That I would be going full-fledged into another decade of servant leadership was unimaginable. Yet, I thought, *Since God wants me to work fully for Him now, I will obey.* After all, He is the One who has brought me to this point and has preserved my life.

But, before entering another ten years of service to the church, I was able to experience, in the first half of 2010, some things that I did so much want to accomplish:

1. Retirement from Colorado's Fourth Judicial District
2. Graduation from Colorado Christian University (CCU)
3. Attend the upcoming SDA General Conference (GC) Session in Atlanta, Georgia
4. Publication of my second book: *Fragrance of God's Love: An Autobiography through the Love of My Friends.*[4]

Retirement

In June 2010, I said goodbye to an aggregate of 44 years of secular employment: eight years with local corporations; twelve years with North American Division of Seventh-day Adventists (NAD); twelve years with the Federal Deposit Insurance Corporation (FDIC), and twelve years with the federal and state judicial systems in the states of Florida and Colorado. My supervisor at the courthouse in Colorado Springs urged me to wait and retire at age 66 (for more income), but I just could not commit to that. I cared more about being free from daily routine commitments, waking up late, and watching the snow—not driving in it—than I cared about making more money. So, retired I was and was happy for that decision. The mediation Office of Dispute Resolution had a large going-away function for me at the El Paso County Courthouse, and many of the mediators, attorneys, judges, and other judicial assistants were present and congratulatory. That day, I almost wanted to rescind my decision to retire, but I was just grateful that my work had been appreciated and that the time had come to depart.

College Graduation

In May 2010, I earned a Bachelor of Science degree in Organizational Management in Christian Leadership from Colorado Christian University (CCU) after a delayed college reentry at the age of 52. At CCU, I was always the oldest in every class, but I was not the smartest—especially in math! My professor bent over backwards and tried to help me with math concepts, while repeating, "Marcia, math, like music, is a universal language, and you must learn the concept." He also reminded me that there were nineteen other students in the class who understood it, and he could not understand why this course in Math Concepts was so difficult for me. I did not know either, but my passion was writing papers—writing anything—and that was all that worked for me. English grammar was my thing, not math. As the other nineteen students moved on in class, seeming to understand everything the professor said, I was struggling. Eventually, I was able to pass the class because a portion of the course required some writing, which was always an easy "A" for me.

During my struggle with Math Concepts, I sought long-distance help from one friend who was (and is) a mathematical engineer. Oops! That did not work. The *light bulb* went on, but I could not see! My son, Eugene, and his wife, Gloria, also tried to help. They had been so happy for me—that after so many years of work and service, I was now able to return to college at night and was finally reaching my goal. When I explained to them how I just could not understand trigonometry and algebra, they took time to come by my condo and *tried* to help me. They used apples, shoes, and whatever type of show and tell to illustrate, and I was so very grateful for their graphic tutelage which assisted in my passing the course. Other than Math Concepts, I enjoyed all of my other classes, especially leadership, research, and psychology classes. Making good grades in those subjects allowed me to graduate with a high GPA.

One of the highlights of having attended CCU was meeting young people who did not know what a "typewriter" was. Another highpoint was meeting "John," one of my military, Catholic classmates. When my first book was published in 2002, *The Complete Wo/Man: An Index to the Heart,*[5] I shared a copy with him. His first comment after reading the book was, "Marcia, you sound just like Ellen G. White!" Then he added, "You know, I have several of her books." This was such a surprise to me. I took his remarks as a compliment and was glad that my classmate showed an interest in the writing and that we were both pursuing a course of higher learning through Christian education.

While appreciating all I had learned at CCU and being happy that I had accomplished my goal of admission and graduation from college, I recognized that, as I studied theories of leadership and organization, that was all they were and what was missing was the link to my life experiences. The *theories* were embodiments of what I had already put into practice for the past several years as manager of a non-profit corporation, as a volunteer in the church, and as a volunteer chaplain in the hospital—all without the benefit

of a college education. The analogy of "putting the *cart* before
the *horse*" certainly fits here. Now I was able to mentally connect
leadership styles and concepts to what I had already done through
the guidance of the Holy Spirit. Learning about leadership styles
helped me to identify why leaders with whom I worked operated the way they did. I also benefitted from learning the type of
leadership style I possessed. Leadership was my favorite subject
in college, and I was able to incorporate this knowledge into the
leadership seminars we presented at different churches.

After retirement and graduation, it was time to put away the
briefcases, the schoolbooks, the study guides, and pull out my
suitcases. I was hitting the road and the airways. My first trip was
to meet up with my sister and family in Atlanta, Georgia for the
General Conference of SDA quinquennial session.

2010 General Conference Session

Since I first arrived in the United States as a child, there have been
numerous General Conference quinquennial sessions; they are
the forum for electing world-church officers and voting changes
to policies. But I have only attended two of these sessions in person. The first was the session in Atlantic City, New Jersey, when I
was a teenager, and my second was in Atlanta, Georgia, in 2010.
Both experiences have left indelible impressions on me and great
memories.

At my first session in Atlantic City, I remember sitting in the
back of an exceptionally large building. So large that those on
stage (before technological media advancements and extra-large
TV screens) looked like *ants*. I was then motivated to pray, *Dear
Lord, I would like to meet some of these people someday. Please
make this possible for me, one day, to see them up close. Amen!* God
answered the prayer of a teenager. Years later (in 1976), after
ending my employment at Oakwood University, I was hired as an
Administrative Assistant to two vice-presidents at the GC offices
in Washington, D.C., where those people who had *looked like
ants*, were now my coworkers. General Conference President Neil
Wilson, father of the current GC president, Ted Wilson, was our

world church leader, and my office was just down the hall from his. My memories from there were beautiful. I have always said, and still do say to this day, that this was the shortest but best employment I ever had.

I never attended another GC session until 2010. The real motivation for that trip was that my sister and her husband were traveling from St. Thomas, Virgin Islands, and I wanted to see them. Plus, I was now retired and could stay in Atlanta for as long as I wanted. No more timesheets! I was now my own boss.

So, there we were one Sabbath morning in Atlanta traveling via M.A.R.T.A (Metropolitan Atlanta Rapid Transit Authority) from the suburb where we were lodging to the convention center in the city.

As my sister and I were descending the stairs to board the train, we could hear a choir singing hymns. As we reached the platform, we could see that these were people like us, all heading to the same destination. I said to my sister, "Let us wait for the next train, these people are *crazy*. Don't they know this is a public place? Why are they singing church songs? Let us rush away to the end of the platform and pretend we do not know them!" My sister said, "No, we won't! Let us join in." So, we did. As our train came into the station, the platform singing paused for the screeching sound of the train brakes. Doors opened, people disembarked, and the Adventists and others who were waiting boarded. As soon as the doors closed and the train departed, the singing started again. I could tell that the other M.A.R.T.A passengers thought, as I had at first, *Oh my, these folks are crazy*! However, we were all in for a spiritual treat. The hymns we sang included "When We All Get to Heaven"[6] and "Marching to Zion,"[7] which were heavenly, both in words and melody. That day, and that experience, changed my

> *We could hear a choir singing hymns…. These people are crazy. Don't they know they are in a public place? That experience changed my thoughts about witnessing for Christ.*

thoughts about witnessing for Christ, knowing that God himself orchestrated that brief encounter which may have offended some, but blessed many.

As much as I enjoyed seeing my family at the 2010 GC session, I did not like being in crowded places. So, I vowed not to attend another of these sessions in person. I am glad that the Internet has made it possible for me (and others) to watch the GC sessions on screen. Consequently, I was able to view the 2015 gathering held in San Antonio, Texas, and that was indeed a blessing.

Publishing of a Second Book

One may ask, why write a second book? Well, the impetus came from a suggestion that was made by a very prominent journalist when I sent him the first chapter of *The Complete Wo/Man: An Index to the Heart*[8] for his review and comments. His comments were that the first book should be about one's passion and the second an autobiography. He added that, after that, you may write about anything your heart desires. Thus, my second book, *Fragrance of God's Love: An Autobiography through the Love of my Friends*[9] was written in 2009 and published in 2010. This, my third book, mirrors the two earlier writings, but, as you get deeper into reading this, you will observe numerous differences.

Now that my immediate goals (retirement and graduation) had been reached, it was time to roll up my sleeves and go as God had instructed: to spend my next years as a ministry leader again in His church.

Chapter 3

Never Say Never

Transferring membership from one local church to another in November 2009 was good for me and for the growth and development of the Central Church congregation. This was the crowning blessing of a lifetime in which God wanted me to know, beyond the shadow of a doubt, that He would and did carry me.

Central Church was not unknown to me. I had attended there as a visitor one Sabbath in 2000, and my experience was not a good one. Why? Well, as I entered the foyer of the church building that morning, a lady was about to hand me a bulletin, and when our eyes met, she put the printed program aside and retrieved another sheet of paper. While handing me this paper, she said: "Here is a map to another church in which you may feel more comfortable." Realizing right away that this was perhaps a racial, prejudicial remark, I looked at her very quizzically, then I smiled and said, "I do not want a map; may I have a bulletin please!"

I was very infuriated and hurt that morning as I walked from the foyer into the sanctuary. Surprisingly, I did see (and meet) a lady who *looked like me*. Her name was "Sister Ella." So, I sat with her in that study group and was welcomed. I stayed through the Sabbath School time and sat in the back pew of the church until the service ended. I left immediately after the service, and, while sitting in my car, I vowed that I would *never* return.

However, I did return about a year later. Not for Sabbath service, but during an evangelistic satellite series that was being shown on screen and only at Central Church. This event was in the evening, so I invited a soldier I had recently met to attend with me as she wanted to know more about our church's beliefs, and I did not have time to study the Bible with her. My friend never knew of my previous so-called "bad" experience, and we were not approached in a negative way during those meetings. *This is great,* I thought. *Perhaps since these sermons are shown only on weekday evenings, my new friend and I could slip in and not experience any unfriendly encounters.* Thank God; no one hindered us. We sat in the third pew from the front each evening throughout the series. And my friend, at the end of the series, gave her heart to God and was baptized after transferring to another state. She later married an elder and served with him in the church. That was indeed a blessing!

Now, here I was nine years later (2009), being directed to a place I vowed I would *never* again attend — not as a congregant, and certainly not as a member. God, however, had intentions of rescinding my vow. At this time, my children and grandchildren had already been attending Central Church, and they thought I would love the congregation and the new pastor who had arrived in November 2008 and had been there for just a year: Pastor Mike Maldonado. Even with their encouragement, I was unsure of what was in store for me. It did not matter, however, as I knew God had ordained this move. My main concern and prayer to the Lord was this, *How would I fit in? And, Lord, what do you have in store for me and for them?* Well, it was not long before I understood the ambiance of this new church and that God had been working through this new pastor to bring about unity in diversity and diversity acceptance.

I had met Pastor Mike and his wife Brenda before attending the church. It was one Sabbath when I had been invited to lunch with my son and his family at their home. After leaving Palace of Peace, while on my way to their house, our plan was interrupted. My son called and diverted me to their pastor's home, because they had just received an invitation to dine with them after services. Well, reluctantly, I changed directions and headed to meet them at this new location. Upon arrival, I received a very respectful welcome from the pastor and his wife. Even though I felt a bit uncomfortable because I did not know them, their hospitality and humility were very impressive. At that point, however, I was still a member at the Palace of Peace Church, and God had not yet shown me His transitional plan.

It was approximately a month after meeting the first family of the Central Church that God showed me His transitional plans. So, there I was one Sabbath morning in 2009, beginning an experience that I did not know would last for another decade. I was unaware of what type of reception awaited me. Surprisingly, as I walked up the steps toward the main entrance of the building, there was a couple who greeted me—literally with open arms, beautiful smiles, and expressions of happiness. Later I learned they were retired Pastor Stan Teller and his wife Joann. The second Sabbath I was also greeted by Pastor Stan and he called me by my first name. Wow! I was overly impressed by this.

I believe God used these greetings to settle me into my new church home. Each Sabbath I would sit in the first or second pew of the sanctuary with my children and granddaughters, absorbing and enjoying a different genre of praise music, extraordinary tranquility, and a restful and calm spirit. I felt almost as though this place and the people (whom I did not yet know) were preparing me for heaven. Eventually though, I began to feel disquieted. Why? Well, week after week Pastor Mike kept asking for volunteers, and I just wanted to relax. One Sabbath, while listening to another appeal from him for help, the Holy Spirit quietly urged me to turn around. I felt it would be embarrassing to do that, but eventually I did look behind me. Wow! I saw a sanctuary that easily could have seated 300–400 people and only about 150 or fewer persons were sitting in the pews. I knew the church had recently split and that

> *I was still learning how to pray for myself. I did not feel I could lead out in intercessory prayers for others!*

this new pastor had come to heal and restore but I did not think I would have a part to play in this restoration. When I quickly faced front again, the Holy Spirit clearly spoke to my thoughts, saying, *You are an ordained elder of the church; you need to get up from your seat and help this pastor.*

Subsequently, I contacted Pastor Mike, and we scheduled an appointment to meet at his office. After re-introductions, a little collective history, and vision-sharing, our pastor spoke of the volunteer help he would need: (1) A Prayer Ministry Coordinator, and (2) assistance in obtaining directory information because he wanted to send birthday cards to each regular attendee. *What?* I thought. This man is *off his rocker.* My response to the pastor was, "No, Pastor Mike. This is not what I want to do." Actually, I was still learning how to pray for myself; I did not feel I could lead out in intercessory prayers for others! And sending birthday cards to every attendee sounded absurd to me and too huge a project for one person. (In my mind, I was thinking, *We go to the same church, but this pastor and I are not the same religion.*) What I did not know then was that Pastor Mike had studied the life of Jesus and operated not only from the head, but from the heart. To him, discipling and nurturing believers was just as (or perhaps even more) important as traditional "soul winning."

After my refusal to accept either of these two volunteer tasks, Pastor Mike then asked, "Marcia, what would *you* like to do at Central Church?" Very quickly I responded: "Pastor, I would love to serve in establishing an effective Foyer Ministry." He accepted that; he prayed, and I departed.

Our meeting appeared unsuccessful. As we parted ways, I saw Pastor Mike walking across the parking lot; his shoulders appeared slumped, and he looked extremely disappointed. Feeling quite guilty and not knowing what to do, I called my best friend (my human panacea), Betty Jean Anderson in Florida and shared my chagrin. Of course, I should have known there would be no sympathy emanating from Betty. After listening to my story and my feelings of embarrassment and disappointment, she said, "Marcia, flesh and blood did not speak through your pastor. It was the Holy Spirit." Wow! Her response to my quandary was gut wrenching. My guilty complex for not accepting Pastor Mike's proposal disappeared as I was now convicted by her words. I, almost immediately, called the pastor and stated that I had reconsidered and would volunteer as Prayer Ministry Coordinator and Card Ministry Facilitator—provided that I could still be creative in developing a plan for the Foyer Ministry. He was accepting, and we started diligently working together.

At the beginning of this chapter, it appeared that Colorado Springs Central Church in the year 2000 was a separate and exclusive group of Caucasians, but as I soon discovered, this was quite to the contrary. First of all, the Palace of Peace Church (a predominantly African-American congregation) and other groups were born out of the Central Church congregation. Also, when I became a member in 2009, I was fully accepted as a leader with no obvious disdain. During my subsequent ten years of service, the membership grew not only in number, but we became a multi-cultural worship center that embraced many ethnic diversities.

Pastor Mike best described this transition in an article he wrote for the Rocky Mountain Conference of SDA *News Nuggets* in July 2020, entitled "From Mono-ethnic to Multi-ethnic: One Church's Journey."[10] With permission I have included this article.

"From Mono-ethnic to Multi-ethnic: One Church's Journey"

It has been said that a church should reflect the demographic of its community. If a community is mainly Caucasian, then it is no fault of the church if its members are mostly Caucasian. But if a church is in a racially diverse community and the demographic is mainly Caucasian then there is work to be done. That is the situation my wife and I found ourselves in in 2008 when we first arrived in Colorado Springs to pastor Central Church.

Colorado Springs is a diverse community due to the large military presence, numerous universities and colleges, a booming economy, and a red-hot housing market. Yet for the most part, Central Church was mostly Caucasian with little diversity. I do not believe Central's "whiteness" (for lack of a better word) was due to prejudice or overt racism but rather from a lack of diversity-oriented leadership in the past. The bottom line is the leader of an organization or church creates the culture and values of the organization.

When my wife Brenda and I arrived in Colorado Springs, we were welcomed with open arms, mainly because the church had been without a pastor for almost a year! I do not think they realized the implications of having a pastor born in Mexico and a pastor's wife born in Nicaragua (and being one quarter Chinese)!

One of the core values my wife and I have is that racial diversity is a beautiful thing. It does not matter in what area you live, having a mix of cultures and ethnicities always makes life more fun and beautiful. We gained these values from having lived overseas for a period of time, traveling extensively around the world, and my wife's two dozen medical mission trips to places such as Kenya, Uganda, South Sudan, Venezuela, Columbia, Greece, Iraq, and many more.

When we arrived at Central, the standard practice when a person of color showed up was to let them know (out of courtesy, of course) that there was a Black church, Korean church, Hispanic church that they might like to try out. We even had directions to the other churches printed out for them! I immediately stopped this practice. We made sure that the greeters did not send people of color to other churches but let them know they were welcome at Central. Up front I verbalized again and again that all people were welcome at Central regardless of race or ethnicity. But it was not just about race, we also let people know that anyone, no matter what their background or history, was welcome. Our vision for the first nine years was simply to create a safe place for all people to come and grow spiritually together. It took time but word eventually got out that Central had changed!

Two other big steps in transitioning from an all-white church to one more reflective of the community was International Sabbath and Brenda's mission reports. Once a year we host an International Sabbath where we have a guest speaker from another country, plus the service is done in various foreign languages and we encourage members to come dressed in their national dress. It is now our most popular service, mainly because of the international lunch after worship! In addition, every time Brenda went on a mission trip she always came back and gave an inspiring mission report/sermon. She has awakened the congregation to the beautiful diversity in the world and brought it back to Central Church.

We were also very intentional about bringing diversity into our leadership team. Eleven years later it is remarkable to experience the diversity at Central. The senior pastor is Mexican, the head elder is Caucasian, the associate pastor is Samoan, the secretary is from British Virgin Islands, our Bible worker is Jamaican, and our school board chair is African American…. There are still a few pockets of resistance in the church but with love, education, strong leadership and the softening of the Holy Spirt, walls of prejudice and fear are coming down and the banner of Christ is being raised high above the nations! —Pastor Mike Maldonado, Central Church

Chapter 4

First, a Volunteer

B y now you must have guessed which of the volunteer ministries was immediately embraced. Yes! Foyer Ministry. This affinity grew after my first, second, and third greeting experiences at Central—one *bad* experience, and two *good*—as detailed in Chapter 3. The bad experience, of course, I never wanted to repeat, and the good was a perfect example of what I sought to facilitate! Before assuming the tasks in the foyer, however, I prayed and asked God to give me discernment and help me to carefully communicate our purpose and mission to those joining the team. And always, before leaving home to serve, I would pray for the Holy Spirit's presence in the foyer, for our greeters, and for those who would walk through our doors.

Foyer Ministry in Action

At first, many thought that a hostess' job was identical to that of the greeter. But not so. The greeters would welcome, hand out bulletins, and direct first-time attendees to a hostess on duty. The hostesses then would do intake: requesting name(s) and contact information, answering questions germane to the visitors' or attendees' concerns, and directing the worshipper to the area of the building where their needs would be met. As attendance continued to increase, it soon became noticeably clear that this was not a job for just one hostess. So, recruitment began. When prospective team recruits asked, "What is Foyer Ministry?" Laurie Barton (our first recruit) and I were able to answer that it was a combination of greeters and hosts teaming up to welcome all attendees, and it (the process) went a little beyond that.

For example, on Sabbath mornings, the Holy Spirit begins His work in the parking lot where visitors, single parents with children, senior citizens, and others are sometimes escorted up the stairs, through the front doors and down the hall to the various Sabbath School classrooms or directed to washroom facilities. First-time visitors were always blessed by this, and so were we. Whatever the walk-ins' needs were, we would seek to provide satisfactory answers and assure a level of comfort.

On-the-job training was paramount. I learned that there was a technique and a process to this type of delicate ministry—one that does not develop overnight. First, the host or hostess needs to be conscious of, attentive to, and respectful of the attendee walking in. They must be observant of that person's timidity, their anxieties, and their reluctance to share information (sometimes even their name). The host or hostess many times may be unaware of an attendee's emotional state—a personal relationship they have just left or have just gotten into, their present emotional condition, or what has brought them (sometimes driven them) to the house of God. At times we can judge by appearance and verbiage that things are not well with that person. Many times, we have not a clue as to why some first-time visitors have dropped in, but this is not as important as the fact that they *are present*. We see each attendee as a child of God. And, later perhaps, some will share their story if a comfort level is developed between them and one of our spiritual leaders. This usually will occur at dinner, either at a member's home or in our fellowship hall. After Central Church began having guest meals (fellowship meals) every Sabbath, part of our welcome was to inform and invite each first-time visitor to lunch in our fellowship hall after the worship service. Those in leadership would mingle with our guests—getting to know them better and they us. Eating together was a major focus and a great soul-winning endeavor, one in which our pastor was very intentional.

Foyer team members would mention to each first-time visitor who was willing to give their name, e-mail address, and/or telephone number that information shared with us would be kept confidential and only submitted to our pastor and that he would contact them. We assumed many thought *no way!* But we knew it was *yes way!* Over the years I have heard many say they were surprised that, in fact, Pastor Mike did take the time to contact them the very next week. This was an impetus for newcomers to continue attending and eventually choosing to join the church. Many also accepted our invitation to take an active part in ministry because they felt this was a caring church and they wanted to give back.

The foyer became a place where some shared brief comments about their past week—their blessings and disappointments, their need of prayer for employment or for a job for which they have recently interviewed, answers to a specific prayer request, a new job or loss of employment, illness, death of a loved one, etc. You may be wondering, *How can the hostesses remember names and needs of so many?* Well, wonder no more. As you might have guessed, we transcribed this information with a clipboard and writing instrument in hand. We had three pages on our clipboard: one for name and contact information, the second for names of members we had not seen in quite a while who were today present, and the last page held all the requests for prayers and visitation.

There were many times when a distraught attendee wanted prayer, and we had to choose between praying immediately with them or continuing to attend to our primary duty, since other worshippers would be waiting for us to receive them. After consulting with Pastor Mike about how inadequate we felt with these two important, yet conflicting, alternatives, he immediately assigned one or two elders (usually a male and one female) to position themselves in the foyer as well, to pray with those needing immediate intercession. This was a great blessing!

Almost 98% of the time after the service, if not praying with someone up front, our pastor would meet and converse with parishioners as they exited the building. Then, he and Brenda would continue their *friendship ministry* in the fellowship hall during lunch. There were times when they (especially Pastor) did not make it to lunch because families living far away waited to meet with him after service, and he would accommodate and minister to them.

As the hostess team made contact from week to week, it was not easy trying to remember everyone's name, but eventually it was a *breeze*. And unbeknownst to me, Pastor Mike's memory was off the charts. Not only did he remember names of adults, but he also knew the names of all the children—even the babies. One thing we had to be careful of was that every name given us was spelled correctly, and whenever we heard an unfamiliar name (or a familiar one for that matter), we knew to not only ask for the spelling but the pronunciation as well. Then we would write the phonics next to the name for Pastor Mike. After his first contact with newcomers, our pastor was able to call each by name and pronounce each name correctly. But what was really pressuring to us is that he expected elders, department leaders, greeters, and hostesses to call each person by name after his or her first visit, as well. (And he definitely wanted me to remember as well in case he viewed someone from a distance whose name he was not sure of. Talk about pressure!) Usually, though, I would remember the adult's name and he would remember the child's or children's name. When this happened a few times, it made me smile because I knew God was using this position to keep my brain cells active. Our Father is so amazing!

After a while, it became evident to all that the Pastor and leaders who mingled with new people on Sabbaths knew the names of almost everyone, but, because of our rapid growth, many congregants did not know each other. Then, Hostess Laurie came up with the idea of "Name-tag Sabbath." And every second Sabbath of the month, there was a table in foyer with name tags on which attendees wrote their names and promised to wear the tags while in the building. This was really helpful, and made it possible for worshippers, when greeting each other, to be able to identify the faces of individuals and families and recall their names.

It was not always easy to link names with faces, especially of those who attended irregularly. One example of this was because

Colorado Springs was a military town. Those soldiers who attended our church were usually present every other weekend but sometimes not for months because of training. This made it a bit difficult at first to match the names with the faces when they would return. However, those whose families remained in our city and attending church weekly—in spite of their soldier's training and/or deployment— kept us connected and informed. What was really helpful to the leaders as they tried to remember the names of our soldiers and their families was having access to our pictorial directory and seeing a picture of the soldier with his or her civilian family members. This pictorial directory, as a way to stay connected with families who were stateside, was, and remains, another tool in helping us to stay connected with our members in a more caring way.

Servant leadership as a lead hostess at Central Church was incredibly challenging, rewarding, and humbling. This position was:

- Challenging because it was something I had never done, and strategies had to be developed during the process. Plus, I missed sitting in the pews. It was tough being on the outside of the sanctuary and not joined with congregants in singing, prayer, praise, and worship—and not even hearing a sermon (even with monitors in the foyer).
- Rewarding because I was able to go home after church and watch the entire service on the Internet (on my big screen TV) and enjoy every moment as a congregation of one. And, as I watched over the Internet, I took pride in the fact that my son, Eugene, was the original engineer of this Internet broadcast access from Central Church.
- Humbling in many, many ways, but the following story stands out for me, and I will share this with you:

It was one Sabbath when the church was open all day. There was a community event being held at our venue in the afternoon, and I was the hostess for that evening. After interacting with first-time visitors and others in the fellowship hall during lunch, I returned to the foyer and observed pieces of paper on the carpet and also that the ladies' restroom trash had not been emptied.

Wow! I immediately switched gears and went into clean-up mode. With a plastic trash bag of soiled paper towels in one hand, I began picking up pieces of paper from the front area; an attendee to the evening program had arrived early and, as our eyes met, I observed an incredibly surprised look on her face. Without even saying, "Hello," she asked, "Elder Armstead, I heard you had left the Palace of Peace Church; are you the janitor at Central Church now?" Her question caught me off guard, and I wanted to answer, "No," as fast as I could, but the Holy Spirit said, "Do not give her your answer; let her receive mine." (Wow! Thank you, Jesus!) My answer through the Holy Spirit was, "I and others are in leadership roles at Central Church, and whatever needs to be done in God's house, we all do." Then I smiled quite genuinely. She smiled as well, and we hugged.

> *All credit goes to Our Father in Heaven, the Holy Spirit's guidance, and the undying love of Jesus for all mankind!*

I believe Foyer Ministry is just as important as pastoral ministry and, in fact, they go hand in hand, and the Holy Spirit's guidance is needed for each. Preparing to represent Him each Sabbath was a must, as it was extremely evident that this was my *calling*; it was also a fantastic introduction to pastoral "Friendship Ministry," as Pastor Mike labeled all areas of people-nurturing that occurred.

It has been a blessing to work with a foyer team that exemplifies God's love. It is my conviction that every church, large or small, that has one minister or many, can be blessed with this type of inclusion and nurturing outreach.

As lead hostess for ten years, I witnessed an increase in church membership which can be credited to the following: Pastor Mike's preaching and teaching; the servant-leadership style that he and his wife exhibited; the attentiveness of Central Church's greeters, hosts, elders, deacons, and deaconesses; and to our continual spiritual growth and attentiveness to Christian duty. But, in fact, all credit goes to Our Father in Heaven, the Holy Spirit's guidance, and the undying love of Jesus for all mankind!

This chapter probably could have been entitled, "Keys to Church Growth" because what we may consider just a humble volunteer position was indeed one of the keys used to usher some lost souls into the kingdom of God.

Prayer Ministry Lessons

Absolutely no church congregation, no leader, and no family member can live happily, effectively operate, and survive spiritually, physically, or economically without God's leadership. It is through our prayers that we reach the throne of God. And, to our requests, He responds. The power of spiritual efficacy only comes from God; and, the man or woman, boy or girl, who does not pray, trust, and obey, will not receive marching orders from above.

Accepting the Prayer Ministry Coordinator position at Central Church was going to be a trial weighing upon my stamina and lack of experience in this area. However, I believed this task would not only fulfill a corporate necessity but also a personal need. In 2010, we started out by establishing a small Prayer Ministry team. Our first attempt at sparking a genuine interest in united prayer was an all-night prayer service conducted at the church, utilizing small rooms decorated to create an atmosphere for prayer and meditation. Several were in attendance, and the undertaking seemed to have gone well, but I had to admit some inadequacies as a prayer leader. I was yet unprepared and unskilled for what could have been an immensely powerful event. Interest was not lacking, however, and I believe our pastor sensed that, too.

True to his word and anxious to elevate this ministry to a high level of success, Pastor Mike started equipping me with resources and exposure to prayer conferences. He suggested I attend a local prayer weekend in Canon City, Colorado, where Ruthie Jacobsen, then General Conference/North American Division (GC/NAD) Prayer Ministry Director, was a speaker. Four of us attended (including my friend Carletta and her mother). After this conference, I came away with some more ideas on how to lead in this capacity and also with a desire not to give up and to keep moving forward. But I had a long way to go to acquire the full self-confidence needed for this ministry. One thing that I did come away with from this conference was a suggestion that Prayer Team members wear "May I Pray for You" buttons. So, not long after, we found a novelty store that manufactured buttons with that saying. Some of us would wear the pins on Sabbaths at church, and attendees were motivated to ask us to pray. One day, while mailing a package at the USPS (United States Postal Service), the attendant, in the process of giving me my change kept saying, "Yes." "Yes." "Yes." This was very puzzling, and I asked why he was saying, Yes"?. He responded, "Yes. Please pray for me." I was unaware that I had a button on my jacket that asked the question. I prayed for him and also realized that this was working not only at church but it could be a ministry to wear these pins in the community as well.

There were members at Central Church who really wanted to see this ministry succeed. Two individuals kept giving me books to read and sometimes would ask, "Marcia, have you read *this* book?" I know they were trying to be helpful, but the more books they presented, the more inadequate I thought I must have been. In order to conquer this concern of inadequacy, I began praying more and more for God to resolve this dichotomy, and He did just that—through another prayer conference.

It was in January 2012. Our church sponsored me to attend an NAD prayer conference weekend near Tarpon Springs, Florida. It was spectacular! Not only did we receive a wealth of teachings, spiritual nourishment, and great encouragement, but I was personally renewed, extremely blessed, and Christ-confident. I will share three experiences from that weekend that changed my life and strengthened my faith forever.

First, as participants gathered in the large conference room on that beautiful Florida Friday evening, to begin our prayer session, a gentleman sat near me. We acknowledged each other and exchanged first names. At a time when the attendees knelt to pray in twos, we prayed for one another. I still did not know who this gentleman was until the next day when he presented as one of the guest speakers at the conference. To my amazement, I had dialogued and prayed the night before with Pastor Pavel Goia. As the audience listened to his praises and testimonies regarding answers to prayer and the *miracles* that had happened in his life as a result of his relationship with God, I was inspired and motivated (more than ever) to become a prayer warrior. And I was anxious to return to Colorado Springs and make a difference in our church. There were many other great speakers at this gathering, but the Goia testimonies were what I personally needed to hear. They changed my prayer life and improved my effectiveness in servant leadership.

Secondly, there are and always will be personal blessings as well whenever we say, "Yes" to doing for God and for others. My personal blessing happened on the Sunday morning before leaving the assembly. As my friend, Betty Anderson, and I stood in the foyer perusing display tables and getting ready to say our goodbyes (she was on her way back to Orlando and I was going to visit friends in Tarpon Springs), we saw walking toward us someone I did not realize had been in attendance at the conference. He was someone I had considered a long-time friend, whose trust I had unknowingly betrayed almost thirty-four years before. During the intervening years, we had seen each other (had even been in each other's homes) and passed each other during small and large church gatherings, but there was always *an elephant in the room* each time we met. (An enormous controversial *faux pas* had made us uncomfortable in each other's presence.) Initially, we had spoken on the phone after the incident occurred. I had expressed how sorry I was and wondered if he could or ever would forgive me, but I never received that forgiveness.

For years we had not spoken about the subject. But I prayed that, before either of us died, the "elephant" would die. Well, it happened at this prayer conference in Florida. As our eyes met, he smiled warmly, and so did I. Then he took the time to congratulate me on my book, which he had read, and I also complimented him on his book and added that I had quoted some of his material in my seminar presentations over the past few years. There were no words spoken about the earlier incident and the many years of ambiguity and strain. However, from the jubilation and smiles and expressions on both our faces, the Holy Spirit revealed that all *was* forgiven. This was one of the greatest moments in my personal life that reassured me that God heard my prayer and knew my heart, and so both our prayers were answered. My friend and I have since communicated, but we live thousands of miles apart and may never see each other again on this earth, but I pray we will be friends, not just on Facebook, but in heaven. God loved me enough to answer my prayer of thirty-four years. Praise His Holy name!

The third personal gratification I received by attending this NAD prayer conference was that I was able, before flying out the next day, to stop by and see some friends: Wilton and Jennifer Lee, while reuniting with their son (and my godson) "T.J." This family and other friends that my late husband and I knew when he pastored the Clearwater Bethlehem Church were present at their house: Minnie Lee, Betty Lee-Hogan, Al and Mary Lee, and T.J.'s siblings. Of course, all knew in advance that I was in town, and a get-together was planned. It was a beautiful gathering with food, fun, and laughter. We were all so glad to see each other—if only for a few hours. It was a very gratifying visit that concluded this blissful weekend. I flew back to Colorado Springs, praising the Lord every step of the way and with a stronger, more fervent, belief that God truly answers prayers. He may not come through when we think He should, but He does at His appointed times.

Often when one returns from a prayer conference, the sponsor (the church) wants to know, "How was it?" However, this will always be a question that cannot be adequately addressed. Yes, you may say, "It was great!" "Wow. We had a nice time!" "Everything was perfect!" But these are just mundane responses to routine questions. The result of a prayer conference cannot be *reported*. It has to be *experienced*! It is a phenomenal happening. It is Spirit led, Spirit generated, and it cannot be transferred or duplicated. I have found that attendees cannot truly communicate their experiences. The only way the church as a whole can benefit is through visible, demonstrative changes reflected through servant leadership. There will (or should) be an overflow or an outgrowth of the Holy Spirit from the one who represented the church, bringing feedback through effective (timely and loving) administration.

After returning to Colorado Springs from the Florida prayer conference, our local church implemented some initiatives that included the following:

(1) Forming a prayer team to include the pastor, elders, department heads, Sabbath School teachers, and a few selected prayer team members who also possessed a sincere passion for united prayer to assist in prayer events: decorating, cooking, and participating in programs and devotionals,

(2) Distributing a prayer list every week to this prayer team and informing via e-mail of emergency requests that surfaced during the week,

(3) Encouraging and forming a prayer group that prays telephonically, for an hour, every Tuesday evening through a free conference call, giving not only the prayer team but homebound individuals an opportunity to call in as well,

(4) Starting a United Prayer Breakfast, the third Sabbath of each month that was open to people within the community, and

(5) Having an annual "Five Nights with the King" meeting—with guest speakers (or elders and youth in the church) preaching nightly.

By the way, "Five Nights with The King" is not original, but it came from the lips of an eight-year-old named Amira. She had overheard me speaking with her grandma about doing only five nights (Sunday–Thursday) and questioning what we should call this one-week emphasis, seeing that we would not be meeting for seven nights. Then, Amira said, "Why don't you call it "Five Nights with the King?" And so, it was!

Our Prayer Ministry Department was now more energized and purpose driven than ever before. Their leader's confidence had gotten *a shot in the arm* and the ministry was now supported by many volunteers.

The next and final NAD prayer conference I was privileged to attend was held in Monterey, California (January 2014). This was exciting. My first time in that state, where I was shuttled in a van from the airport to the campus where the meetings were held and shuttled back to the airport after the meetings ended. (So, I can almost agree that I have never really seen California.) Here again, this prayer conference was another marvelous experience that cannot be described in words for anyone to understand but the attendees. There were, however, some great memories, of which I will share a few:

I knew Pastor Mike would also be attending this event. We had never, up to this point, traveled together in the same vehicle or airplane, and this was always a good thing to me because I would wonder, *What if something happened to both of us? What would become of Central Church?* I know; quite vain. Isn't it? Nevertheless, I prayed, "Please, Dear Lord, don't let my pastor and I be on the same flight!" I was departing from COS (Colorado Springs) to DIA (Denver) to meet my connecting flight to California. And, thank God, there was no one I knew who initially boarded with me in COS. However, as passengers were waiting to board the connecting flight at DIA, it was announced that the scheduled flight to California was canceled, and passengers needed to step to the counter for rebooking. While in line for reassignment, I heard someone from behind say, "Marcia, is that you?" I started to laugh as I slowly turned around. That someone was Pastor Mike! When our eyes met, I could see he was, courteously, trying not to laugh. But I did. I laughed for about two minutes straight.

God knew I wanted us to be on separate airplanes, and He answered my prayer, as Pastor Mike and I, thank God, were rebooked on separate flights. How cool was that! On my connecting flight though, I did meet up with a friend, Prayer Warrior Yvonne Grimes, whom I had not seen in years. I was so glad to see her, and, although we did not get to sit together on the trip, it was reassuring to know that she was on board. I was unaware that we would be flying so near to so many mountain peaks to get to Monterey that I almost wished some other person from Central Church would have taken this trip instead of me. Then I was comforted with the thought that Prayer Warrior Grimes was on board and where two or three are gathered together to pray, God answers.

Yvonne and I partnered with each other during the NAD periods of prayer, worship, workshops, and meals. We enjoyed the pleasantness of meeting new people. We fellowshipped with associates, met old friends, and most of all worshipped with NAD conference presenters and listened to great sermons and testimonies. The January 9–12 theme was: "Go to the Rock." The ultimate spiritual experience for me was to participate in congregational prayers and songs that drew the heart into prayer.

It was also good to converse briefly with my late husband's long-time friend and colleague, Pastor David Long, who was among others my family had not seen in a long while. Meeting new people was fun and introducing Yvonne to our pastor was a treat. It was at this gathering that we met Michele Seibel, a dynamic preacher from Hawaii, who took us to the *mountain top* with her message, "Cleft for Me." Again, there are no words to describe the wonders of God's presence and His love that I felt in that sermon.

This particular conference was not about whom we saw or even what we learned. To me, it was about spiritual incentives. While traveling back to COS, it became clear that no matter the task assigned to any child of God, there are rewards. For me, this prayer ministry conference was God's spectacular gift of a vacation to me (specifically) for volunteering at Central Church. This trip, being among people of like-mindedness, was a New Year's present in so many ways.

Not only did I benefit, but so would our church. This ministry leader was returning with more fervor and with plans for our team of volunteers at Central Church. While traveling back home on the aircraft, my mind could not rest. So, I started working on new goals and objectives and methods for achieving them. I knew that our leadership desired that we sail beyond being just a church *with* prayer, but we needed to be a church *of* prayer—allowing prayer to saturate (to be woven into and fill) the very fiber of our church body. So, on the plane I wrote down some notes of things that we would continue doing but with a more precise methodology.

Goals and Objectives

My notes became a list that could guide us going forward.

1. Continue accepting prayer requests from those needing prayers, either for themselves or others, and pray daily—individually, with family, or with a prayer partner—for these requests. Follow up with those for whom we are praying to listen to their testimonies of praise and thanksgiving.
2. Have members of our prayer team meet every Sabbath morning in the Prayer Room from 9:00–9:30 a.m. to pray for immediate needs, for sanctuary services, for our pastor, for others ministering to the congregation, and for all activities in our building and community.
3. Be more intentional in encouraging others to attend mid-week Prayer Meetings, as well as praying in groups, and praying for one another whenever and wherever possible.
4. Continue our monthly United Prayer Breakfast every third Sabbath.
5. Continue planning, with church leadership for the annual Fall Week of Prayer in September or October that would feature "Five Nights with the King—KIDS," in which the children in our school, Springs Adventist Academy, and those in our Children's Ministry Department, would be involved.
6. Conduct a Prayer Team meeting at least once per quarter.

As the Prayer Ministry Department at Central Church became more active and purpose driven, Pastor Mike had a desire to create a prayer room. But where? All the rooms in our building were earmarked for essential activities! But, because our pastor believed wholeheartedly that a place of prayer in the building was paramount, he called our head elder, Alan Brass and myself together for a meeting and stated that he had been thinking to convert the church library into a prayer room. And why not? The library had been somewhat inactive for quite a while—with no one really checking any materials in or out; and secondly, we could move the books to shelves in our resource room and operate from there. Well, after thoughtful consideration and prayer, this change was agreed upon, and so it was. We now had a prayer room adjacent to the foyer area where consulting takes place, prayer needs are addressed, and issues resolved in a private fashion with those of our pastoral team. On issues needing pastoral follow-up, we suggest that the individual(s) contact our pastor at a later time for a counseling appointment. Many tears have been shed in that room; many prayers have been prayed and souls comforted; and many praises have been received before, and after, God answered prayers.

I remember times when I would consult with a female and then ask, "Is Pastor Mike aware of this?" Some would reply, "Yes, he is, but I wanted to get a female perspective." Another would say, "No, he does not know about this problem; he is a male, and I cannot share this issue with a man." These consulting periods with the women of our church made me even more conscious of the need and importance of having females on the pastoral and leadership team. Women serving women is a necessity in any church and those female leaders are equipped with a God-given passion to deal with sensitive issues that may be difficult for a man. It was so gratifying and helpful that, when I came to Central Church, there was already a female elder in place—Elder Sandy Shute. Sandy was, and still is, a woman with a depth of concern about ministry in general and especially as it relates to the older and homebound members of

When God's people pray, He answers. When they intercede, He acts. And when they praise, He honors.

Central Church. I have been blessed to be associated with her in providing communion to homebound members, but also receiving her help when I had a personal medical issue. She is a Bible teacher at heart and is also a powerful prayer warrior.

Over the next months and years, Central Church's Prayer Ministry team quantified its effectiveness by learning and adopting the theory that prayer essentially is more about caring than praying. In this work I learned that it is not enough to just say, "I will pray for you" or "I have prayed for you." It is also asking yourself or asking the person, "What can I do besides pray?" or "What do you need us to do for you?"—and then fulfilling those requests as much as we can.

In my four and a half years as Prayer Ministry leader, Daniela Dumitru was my prayer partner and chief assistant. After I left this volunteer position, Daniela was Spirit-led to assume the leadership. And she added to the ministry by having group prayers in front of the altar after church for anyone needing prayers. She also increased our involvement with the "Ten Days of Prayer" every January, and she hosted our weekly telephone prayer sessions. Daniela also came up with the idea of producing a video for our website that emphasized our prayer engagements and activities at the church.

Prayer Ministry in any church is a practice that must receive constant attention and commitment to benefit the entire church and its community. So it was, and is, at Central Church. Numerous prayers have been prayed and answered, and I reiterate my belief that, when God's people pray, He answers. When they intercede, He acts. And when they praise, He honors.

Card Ministry

Even though this was the first church and first pastor I had known who sent birthday, condolence, get-well, and congratulatory cards to individuals, we gave it a try. What I discovered was that this IS evangelism! Or what is really called *nurturing*. It warms the heart of those receiving this type of acknowledgement. It is only <u>one</u> way of showing that the pastor cares and remembers each person and family.

It takes more than one volunteer to keep up with this ministry; but, when properly coordinated, it works! It was good to discover that we had a member, Karen McCallister, whose hobby was making cards, and she wanted to be a volunteer by joining the team. Some members, instead of throwing away cards they no longer wanted to keep, donated portions of beautiful birthday (and other) cards to Karen and Central Church's Card Ministry. Former church office secretaries Linda Popejoy, Shannon Perez, and Ola Trotter, provided birthday lists, prepared labels of Scriptures for the inside of those cards and mailing labels for the envelopes. From year to year, card mailings were continuous, as DeNita Wilson and Bethan Clarke joined in to effectuate the preparing and mailing of cards and packages. DeNita and her volunteers also prepared APO (Army Post Office) boxes for servicemen and women and mailed them in a timely manner.

Not only were birthday cards regularly sent out, but get-well, condolence, and congratulatory cards were sent to church attendees and their family members. Cards were also sent to those we knew (and did not know) who were incarcerated. Also, whenever there was news of anyone in our conference needing encouragement or uplift, our pastor had special cards for them as well. Crazy? That is what I thought at first, but the impact of such a personal touch is rare and had exceptional results.

Over the years, several other assignments were added to my list of volunteer activities, but the success achieved and blessings realized in guiding and helping in these three initial tasks— hosting, prayer leadership, and card ministry—was a win-win for me personally, for those we served, and for the growth and unity of Central Church.

Chapter 5

Chosen, Qualified, Valued

T he first three years at Central Church as a volunteer were stimulating. I got to know the members and their families, meet new attendees, develop strategies, and earn the respect and love of the majority of the congregation. Gradually, our internal focus on the needs of our members and listening to their family struggles, propelled me beyond the walls of the church.

Beyond the Walls

I found myself being more involved with the congregation and being more of a go-to-person, which I loved. I was actively involved in doing community research; making appropriate referrals; advocating for some who were involved in litigation; and visiting those who were ill in their homes, in hospitals, and in rehabilitation centers. As this outreach expanded, I had now placed myself in a more elaborate and representative role. At times, when Pastor Mike was overwhelmed and unable to be in two places at once— because of a wedding; a funeral; a court appearance; being out of town or country (which was very rare); or attending an obligatory conference session; he would call on me or our head elder, Alan Brass, as a backup when there was an urgent matter involving the saints.

I have had the privilege of knowing and working with Elder Alan Brass and his beautiful wife, Dianne. Alan was the head elder at Central Church when I arrived and still is at the time of this writing. He is the BEST head elder I have ever known. My wish after meeting and knowing this family is that every church, every pastor, ought to have such a "right hand" person and family in their midst. After observing his leadership style and the concerned, personable attitude that exuded to everyone around him, I would, now and then, do some subjunctive reflection, *What if my late husband had had an assistant such as this man?* The sky would have been the limit to their progress. Pastor Maldonado, and our church, have truly been blessed with this anointed and appointed man of God.

Ethics prevent me from mentioning all the wonderful things we know about Alan and his service, but I will say just two things: First, he reminds me of Jesus *the problem-solver.* He is the go-to man for solutions to overly sensitive church family issues. One Sabbath, as he and Dianne were being honored for fourteen years of service, one of his brothers-in-law, Robbin Barton, said of them: "Many nights my sister sits at home alone, praying for Alan as he attends a *somebody-done-somebody-wrong* meeting." And this categorization received unanimous agreement with those who knew and worked closely with this minister of God.

Secondly, since Alan is not being painted as perfect, I must mention my pet peeve with this "preacher's kid (PK)." Alan's late father was a pastor, and pastors' kids receive many undeserved projections of how they should act or whom they should be or become. Some may have expected him to become a preacher himself. However, in the eleven years I have known our head elder, I have never heard him preach a sermon—only just a eulogy, and that was just once in a great emergency. Therefore, it was a running joke when our pastor would be away, and I had to speak for him, and I would say, "I am filling in today for Elder Brass." After a while, I had to stop saying that, as I realized it was not funny to Alan. God gave me peace with it and only heaven will reveal why this son of a preacher did not like to preach—seeing that he is an excellent extemporaneous speaker. He can easily speak "off-the-cuff," and anything he is asked to say at the last minute rolls off his tongue spontaneously in the most eloquent and graceful (and sometimes funny) way. But he will not preach!

Alan and I worked together well in the field, answering some emergency assignments. As a ministering duet, I remember well visiting homes together where a loved one had died. There were two separate incidents in which a husband and father had died while Pastor Mike was out of state. It was not a problem for me to be of comfort to mothers and widows, but I was not very proficient when ministering to young children. However, both Alan and Pastor Mike worked closely with the youth and had an excellent rapport with them. For these two emergencies, I prayed that Alan would be reachable and available, and he was! Had he not been present, I could have handled the visits, but the Holy Spirit had him there on these occasions to provide the extra support that was needed for these families. Having backup when life is in disarray during grief and sorrow is invaluable. Alan's ministry was supported by his wife, and I knew her as someone who smiled a lot; was very complimentary; and was incredibly supportive of her husband, her church, and her family. They are indeed an amazing couple!

As I grew in knowledge and self-confidence in almost every area of leadership, it become more and more evident that God had indeed prepared me for these routine and sometimes impromptu assignments. He developed my skill set— through the experiences I had had as a former pastor's wife, consultant, a judicial assistant, a chaplain, a single parent, and a grandparent—to understand and serve others.

The importance of my service to the church was apparent to church leadership. Pastor Mike suggested several times that I accept a salary for my services; however, for months I kept refusing this offer. I felt that since my income covered all my present financial needs and that the more I gave the more I received, then there was no need to be financially compensated. But there came a time when my expenses had suddenly increased and I called Pastor Mike and asked if his offer was still open, and there was a positive response.

Within just a few days, I was offered a position by the Rocky Mountain Conference as an Assistant for Pastoral Care at Central

Church. This title was conferred in February 2015. I could not (and would not) have the title of "Assistant Pastor" since I was not in pursuit of a pastoral degree. I had seen a pastor's job from both sides of the spectrum and, even though I respected this profession, it was not on my to-do list. So, after six years of volunteering, I became a staff member at Central Church.

Before my hiring was confirmed, however, our local Church Board had to approve this addition to the staff. The vote passed the Board that evening and, after the meeting was adjourned, a very prominent department leader asked if he could speak with me. As we stood in the foyer of the building, this gentleman expressed to me that I did not receive his vote because he refused to serve under a woman pastor or be ministered to by a female. Wow! This statement was 90% more surprising than it was crushing. I expressed to him that his position was well taken, and I also explained that I would not be "pastoring" the church, just assisting Pastor Mike as I had always done and that was all. I emphasized that I would only be *assisting in pastoral duties*. After this reiteration, this gentleman's position remained the same, and we parted. I was extremely grateful for his candor. I do not know if others who voted affirmatively actually felt the same way, but I appreciated the forthrightness of this leader. He gained my sincere respect that evening.

I am sharing this encounter because this leader was honest, and I was really not offended. God refused to allow me to have any hidden emotional response to his honesty. As a matter of fact, I was somewhat blessed by it and thankful to know that, even though the church board approved this "title," I could continue my tasks with God as My Leader and know that not everyone would be accepting. Little did this leader and I know how God would work with us and through us. But the result was a blessing.

You see, not long after our exchange, and surprisingly, this gentleman and his wife were the first family to request a private consultation in my office. They became two of my most ardent supporters. God had broken down the barriers, and we grew in faith, through prayer, and experienced greater love and admiration for one another.

Chosen

It is without any doubt that I knew God had chosen me to be the Assistant for Pastoral Care at Central Church. Through dreams and signs, He had given me enough knowledge of His works. Was I hesitant? Yes! Unassuming? Yes! But, fearful? Not at all. I relied on what Jesus said in John 15:16: "Ye have not chosen me, but I have chosen you, and ordained you, that ye should go and bring forth fruit, and that your fruit should remain: that whatsoever ye shall ask of the Father in my name, he may give it you (KJV).

> *Our Father knew that, through the stages of my life's work and experiences, He was molding me for this new decade.*

Our Father knew that, through the stages of my life's work and experiences, He was molding me for this new decade. Not because I had achieved a Master in Counseling or a Master of Divinity degree, but because I was just an ordinary person who repented of my sins, had been forgiven, and now was called to serve others under His dictates.

Qualified

Since God had prepared, directed, and commissioned me in ministry, qualification was never a concern for me. And my job description had not actually changed. However, some of the activities in which I was already involved became more inclusive. There was now more awareness of time-sensitivity, protocol, and reporting processes.

While the quality of ministerial work remained the same, some things were different. For example, attention to duty was intensified in that when attendees or staff could not immediately locate the pastor within minutes of their voice message, the next person to contact would be yours truly—but, thank God, this happened very infrequently. Also, I was no longer my own boss. Now, I had to report, not just to the church, but to the conference.

Nevertheless, I was elated to have been given this title and was welcomed by RMC leaders—many of whom prayed for me.

All clerical responsibilities were embraced with self-confidence, even though I had different levels of self-assurance with each:

- Visitation—no problem
- Bible teaching—a breeze
- Renewal of wedding vows—a joy
- Funerals—a challenge
- Dedicating babies—a blessing
- Advocating for litigants—a privilege
- Baptisms—I did not have to do this
- Preaching—by God's grace
- Communion for those who were homebound—satisfying
- Nursing Home Visit Coordinator—insightful.

Visitation was at the top of my list because this was more extensive and intensive than my other duties. Some visits were by appointment, some (especially to hospitals) were urgent or impromptu, and other visits were routine and as needed. There are many precautions and/or procedures one needs to know before visiting with the sick. These include a pre-visit inquiry with the patient or spouse, or verifying with a close family member if unable to reach the patient, or checking with the hospital or rehab center. The nurses at the nurses' station can sometimes give limited disclosure of information, such as letting you know if a patient can receive visitors and/or if he or she has just been discharged or transferred. A pre-knowledge of condition, such as communicable diseases, emotional health issues, ADLs (activities of daily living) is, in most cases, extremely necessary when you are visiting and, of course, all visits should be brief and meaningful.

Usually, when someone was scheduled for surgery, I always wanted to get to the hospital and pray before the procedure. But, if that was not possible, I would go to the hospital in the hours after the surgery or perhaps the next day. (When patients are coming out of anesthesia and/or just getting back to their room, they are just beginning to recover—emotionally as well as physically.)

My chosen method was to visit (at most) a day or two later, unless otherwise summoned.

What I did learn when visiting is that our male members, especially when they are hospitalized, often prefer when a male person visits with them. So, Pastor Mike or Elder Brass would be the ones to do the majority of these visitations. I loved visiting with the women, and I believe they enjoyed me being with them as well.

Bible Teacher. This assignment was extremely easy, especially when I could utilize source material from already published Bible lessons. Having the answers to students' questions, either directly from the Bible or from undisputable commentaries on the different subjects, made for a rewarding interaction with the students. Watching Bible students learn and hearing their views and comments, of what was new to them, was motivating. Some had not read or understood the Bible before, and they expressed their regrets for having lived by only what they heard or what was taught to them by leaders who had misinterpreted or ignored biblical truths. I loved this weekly gathering.

Pastor Mike made the classes even more exciting by creating the Central Bible Institute after the first graduating class in 2018. We used the Amazing Facts Bible series, Lessons 1–27 and, between Lesson 14 and 15, we inserted a study on the Book of Daniel. As we advanced in those studies, there were times when students posed questions for which I had to do additional research in order to give a concrete answer during the next class. At those unique times, I would call one of my friends, Roger Lindo, and dialogue with him on my answer to the question to see if he was in agreement or could add further clarification. I have been friends with Roger and his wife Nancy for many years. When our kids were little, both Roger and my late husband were attending Andrews University (AU), and we lived across the street from each other. Roger graduated from AU with a master's degree in religion. I thank God for old friends who are never tired of helping me in my continuing education.

Renewal of Wedding Vows (and marriages) are joyous occasions. Sitting down with a couple, getting to know them more intimately, listening to their stories, and witnessing their love for one another is joy to me! I have been involved in only three such events but will expound on only one.

First, the bad news. A very dear couple had scheduled their vow renewal on a day when our pastor was to be out of the country, and I was designated to do the honors. Of course, I knew we had planned to meet two weeks before, but yours truly was a week behind schedule. As I was stepping away from the church building one Sabbath, I had my mind on my next assignment: renewal of vows for Curtis and Laura Malcolm, which I thought was in two weeks. The lovely *bride* approached me and said: "We haven't heard from you, and I was concerned." I responded, "I will be making two visits to your home this coming week, and I was going to call you tomorrow so we could go over plans for your renewal of vows, etc. The event is in two weeks, right?" When she responded that it was just a week away, next Sunday, I almost had a heart attack. I was so glad she had approached me and questioned my lack of response. We were able to visit the next week and consultation went well.

At the outdoor event on that special Sunday afternoon, the decorations were exceptionally beautiful, the bride and groom and their party looked regal, and the food—catered by a family member and my friend, Sandra Ingram—was exquisite. The weather was sunny with blue skies, and something happened that I had never witnessed before. And here is the good, or better, news. We stood waiting for Laura to make her entrance. She looked so beautiful, it was beyond words. However, as she approached the love of her life (of fifteen years), she began to sob. As we looked on, while her smiling husband delicately and warmly hugged her, we very quickly realized that these were tears of joy. I had never witnessed a bride cry at the very moment she was to renew her vows and for such an extended period of time. Family, guests, and I realized these were happy tears, and all we could do was smile and bask in the joy of her tears. It was a testament to the life they had lived together and the love they shared. Her husband held her until the tears of happiness ended, and everyone was happy for both of them. I will truly never forget this day, and I was glad this couple allowed me to honor them in our pastor's absence.

Funerals. It has been a challenge, and a blessing, to have presided over four funerals in the past two decades. Three as a chaplain and only one while a pastoral assistant at Central Church. This funeral took place on a day when our church was scheduled to have a Communion service. The family had secured with the funeral home on a weekday (Thursday) for the service and Pastor Mike was on board to officiate. He really wanted to do this eulogy, as he had known the deceased, who was a faithful member, Twila Keller [1928–2019], and some members of her family for a long time. At the very last minute, the mortuary changed the date and rescheduled for two days later—on a Saturday. There we were, Pastor Mike and I, trying to decide what to do, as he could not be in two places at the same time. I had participated as an elder in support of Central Church's Communion service, but had never led out in a full-scale congregational service, and I did not want to try. Our Pastor asked the family if they would then allow me to fill in for him at the funeral service.

Twila's two daughters and their spouses were not strangers to me, as I, too, had known them for quite a few years. So, they wholeheartedly consented and so it was. Unfortunately, I was unable to do the graveside, but the deceased's son-in-law was able to fill that spot for me. I was then able to return to Central Church in time to partake of the bread and wine. While I sorrowed for the family (and for Pastor Mike missing this opportunity), I was also honored to perform this clerical duty, and all were blessed.

A Unique Funeral Arrangement: Another story that is so compelling for me to write here is in regard to assisting with funeral arrangements for a widow's son in which God revealed His amazing grace through answered prayers. Her son had died, she was in deep grief for his loss, and she was unable to pay the burial costs. She invited me and a close friend to come to her home and be by her side as she met with the funeral director. This mourning mom was not well enough to go to the funeral home, so the director was coming to the house. I prayed—as I had never prayed before—that the Holy Spirit would go before me and make a way so that this young man could be funeralized with dignity even though the means were slim. As the four of us gathered around this grieving mom's dining table, she stated her financial status to the mortician and to us. Even with some discounting, she just could not come up with the funds. Well, I felt impressed by the Spirit to explain how this woman had worked for many, many years for our church and (with her permission) I revealed some of the areas in this community where she had served. Then this mortician said, "We will do everything for free; you will only have to pay for the death certificates." With that said, her friend consented to pay for the death certificates and (as we had begun) we ended in prayer. As I drove back to the office that day, I was still in awe at this astonishing reward with which God, and God alone, had answered our prayers!

Dedicating Babies. Unlike funerals, the dedication of infants is a blessing. Here newly born humans (not yet conscious of right or wrong) are brought to the house of God by godly, Bible-believing parents to receive an anointing from heaven, much like Mary and Joseph did for Jesus when they brought Him to the temple to be blessed by Simeon (Luke 2:20–32). Only twice in the last decade was this opportunity afforded me, and I loved doing this!

Advocating for Litigants. Providing this service has been a privilege. These visits to the courthouse, and sometimes the jail, time after time, with parties and their loved ones can be frequent and time consuming. Garage parking; feeding meters; transporting a victim of domestic violence from the hospital to a court hearing; waiting (sometimes hours) until a case is called; praying with litigants, guardians, and social workers (before and/or after hearings); collaborating with both plaintiffs and defendants, petitioners and respondents; consoling the parent or sibling of an inmate; writing to inmates; and transporting inmates released from prison—these have never been overbearing for me. As public as these cases are, when it comes to the response of our pastoral team, all cases are private to us.

This particular ministry appears to be one of the most rigorous and daunting tasks in pastoral work, but our pastoral team has enjoyed it! Why? Because we all believe that everyone deserves at least a second chance. We have seen lives changed, families reunited, justice served, cases won, and cases dismissed. We have also witnessed recidivisms but have never given up on an inmate. Through prayer, written communication, and hope, church and family can bring encouragement not only to those who are incarcerated but also to their families.

Baptisms. Never have I baptized. This was not one of the duties God had in mind for me. I know this, and have acknowledged same. While at Central Church, I witnessed many become *new babies* born to Christ through baptism by immersion. We have also experienced the joy of seeing new believers, returning backsliders, and Internet invitees baptized by water and the Spirit of God. This is one of the most glorious services one can ever attend!

Preaching is not my calling; neither is singing or playing a musical instrument. Even though being called on to serve in the capacity of a speaker at my church on some occasions—and being invited to other churches to do the same—it is not within the context of my special giftings. Do not get me wrong; I love being invited to speak about a theme during special-emphasis services, and I am extremely comfortable being a presenter at women's and men's retreats—especially when I have been asked to facilitate The Complete Woman/Man Seminars. However, I am not a preacher!

By the way, speaking of "preaching," I am reminded of a long-time friend and former coworker whom I met in New York City. His name was "Les." We met when he was seventeen (on his first summer job before going into his senior year in high school), and I was 21 and engaged to be married. After getting married and leaving New York City to live in Alabama, I saw Les once again on a return visit to "The Big Apple"—the other name for New York City that we so often use. We never communicated again until forty-five years later when Les found my PO Box address through social media and wrote a letter to me in Colorado. It was such a joy to have received his communication. His telephone number was enclosed, and I called him right away. My friend is a Christian, a husband and father, and a granddad. Our communication for the past few years has been spiritually refreshing. My friend shares uplifting Internet links with me, and I share our church's website Vimeo with him. He commented very positively about one of my sermons, noting how blessed he was and that he had shared it with some of his friends. Of course, I chuckled; when he asked why, I pointed out some imperfections that were upsetting to me after I had seen the video. His response was, "Marcia, I was not focused on the messenger, but on the message."

My friend's response was sobering. Captured by the realization that it is only by God's grace that any woman, man, boy, or girl receives an opportunity and a platform to spread the gospel brought me to repentance. I had to ask God's forgiveness for discounting the presentation of His message. It is displeasing to Our Father when we disrespect His commission and provision. The messenger is only the vessel, but it is God Himself Who takes full responsibility for the efficacy of His Word. All can speak a word for Christ, irrespective of gender, age, ethnicity, position, or arena. We are His mouthpieces.

Communion for the Homebound. This was one of the clerical responsibilities that I had not yet experienced or been required to do. Bringing Communion to hospitals and nursing homes was comfortable and routine for me as a chaplain. However, I was a bit dubious about doing homebound communion for members who had been for years accustomed to the "warmth" of these services in a congregational setting. As I was wrestling with this, the Holy Spirit urged me to ask for His discernment on how best to do homebound services with those of like faith as compared to ministering in an institutional service. Well, I did pray. And, as usual, God answered my prayers.

I had attended home communions with pastors and other elders, but I never conducted the procedure myself. Each time, I would leave a home feeling a bit dissatisfied—as if we had not done enough. This all ended one day in July 2015, when watching (over the Internet) the sixtieth GC Session of the Seventh-day Adventist World Church that was being held in San Antonio, Texas. It was then I learned how this communion to the homebound is effectively done.

The Session showed a video of a female pastor giving communion to a couple in their home, and it satisfied my longing. I discovered what was missing during my earlier experiences: (1) singing prayerful redemptive songs, (2) asking if the family had any prayer requests and praying for those issues, and (3) leaving something behind. Wow! I was so blessed and excited to have been a viewer. Now, I knew how to do this. What was missing in earlier homebound communion services were words to the songs we had sung which have been forgotten by some (even though they knew the tunes). We did not take time to talk about the family or discover what their prayer needs were. And no song sheets or Scriptures (with pretty images) were left at their home.

Almost immediately, I went to my office and started preparing (actually, upgrading) my Communion package. I typed prayerful and inspirational songs and copied this to half-sheets of paper. They were hymns we sing in church on Communion Sabbaths, songs such as "Redeemed!"[11] "There Is a Fountain,"[12] etc. Then biblical readings concerning the Last Supper, the meaning of Communion, the reason we partake, and what Jesus said of the bread and the wine when He supped with His disciples. These were also typed out and printed with beautiful pictures germane to the service. It was rewarding to have implemented a more adaptable and passionate way of ministering this sacred ceremony in a home. It was no longer coming and leaving with a simple prayer. Now there were intercession and printed words of songs and texts that the family and/or couple could reflect upon.

Thank God for this knowledge and the informative and inspirational video played at the GC 2015 session. It was educational and satisfying for me. And I was now fully confident that I and any partner could minister this holy Communion service with pleasure, meaning, and efficacy.

Nursing Home Coordinating. This was another aspect of out-reach ministry. In 2016, a request came into our church office from a local nursing home, asking if Central Church could bring services to their residents one Sunday each month. We gladly accepted this opportunity to minister, and I was privileged to coordinate these visits. What really encouraged me to accept this task was that our minister of music, John Paul Redmon, consented to be our pianist. He also brought in children's choirs, vocal groups, and soloists. John, in spite of his busy schedule, had committed to being present every Sunday afternoon. I did not doubt his commitment (he is a man of his word), but I questioned his availability. You see, Sunday was his busiest ministry day as he also played not just for Central Church on Sabbaths, but also for two other churches on Sunday mornings. However, would you believe that from 2016 to the beginning of COVID-19 Minister Redmon was only absent three times (for his mother's birthdays) or late twice (by five minutes because he had to transport others). Of course, on those weekends when he was away visiting his mom, he provided back-up musicians. We were never without music and devotional thoughts for the residents. Pastor Mike, too, irrespective of his busy weekend schedule and interrupted family time, frequently attended—bringing a Word from the Lord and/or playing his guitar. What commitment! This ministry was in the heart of our church leaders and volunteers. And God blessed us greatly.

Valued

Every member in the body of Christ is needed and should be appreciated and encouraged. Whether one volunteers, is a staff member, or only attends services and special programs, we are all essential and should be valued. A growing and prosperous church heralds adherence to the directives of biblical stories that show the people of God (in both Old and New Testaments) who worked together within the spheres of their abilities and with the special gifting of the Holy Spirit to perfect "the bride of Christ"—His church.

Feeling valued has always been a conscious part of my everyday living because doing one's best is a very uplifting posture. While growing up, my mom would always say to me and my siblings, "Always do the best you can because, when man has done his best, angels can do no more." We did not know exactly where she got this saying, but we never have forgotten her repetitions. This has always reinforced our loyalty and commitment to any project we embraced. So, at the end of every day, I go to bed feeling valued—if not by man, then certainly by God.

> *"God has blessed you with incredible energy and passion. I am so proud of how you have grown into a confident and humble minister.... I pray that you will continue to receive a fresh anointing every day and you live each moment in the power of the Holy Spirit"*
> *—Pastor Mike.*

Now, I must admit that I was (and still am) lacking in technological skills. My excuses: "I was not born in the computer age" and "There were no computers when I was growing up!" Even with family members and friends who are highly technical, and with others my age who are learning and developing their technological skills, I am simply not with the program. My son always reminds me that my computer is not a twentieth century *typewriter*, and that I need to get into the twenty-first century. My answer always is, "But, my keyboard feels just like a typewriter, and I'm comfortable with it since writing is my thing! Plus, I do have a *smart phone*, and I am doing quite well with that even though it is not getting along with me quite well." Excuses! Excuses! Excuses! Sometimes I wish my grandchildren were around so that, among other things, they could help me with technology. Secretly though, I do wish my technical skills were more developed, but then I would just have more things to remember.

Being a part of any workforce team, both volunteers and paid staff, every now and then, desire an objective evaluation of their value to their organization. Not just a pat on the back, but something tangible that reinforces appreciation and value for dedicated service. Many, like myself, whether or not they receive accolades, still perform and are confident that between them and God, all is well.

As it happened, one Sabbath morning right before the service formally began, I was called up front and honored by the church with flowers and handfuls of goodies and treats. Along with these gifts was an envelope with a letter from Pastor Mike. When I arrived home and read his missive, I was blown away. To what extent? Well, far enough to have had the letter engraved on a plaque which subsequently found a place on the wall in my office.

Pastor Mike's letter read as follows:
Sabbath morning, November 5, 2016

Dear Marcia:

It is early morning, and I am given the impossible task to put into words my/our appreciation for you as a minister of the Gospel of Jesus Christ and as a friend and colleague.

When I came to Central eight years ago, I did not know at the time the impossible task that lay ahead, but God did, and He knew I would need a special kind of associate. So, He orchestrated your path and brought you to Central to be my associate much like Aaron was to Moses and Timothy to Paul.

The last seven years will go down as the era of Pastor Mike and Sister Marcia. I am so proud of how you have grown into a confident and humble minister in your own right. You are an accomplished speaker, very articulate, with a good command of the English language. The people love you and easily connect with you. Although you have strict beliefs and standards, you remain so full of love and grace for everyone, no matter how messed up we are.

Despite some health issues and lack of proper funds, you continue to serve our congregation tirelessly and with honor and dignity. You do it all. You visit in the courts, hospitals, hospice, homes, and schools.

You give Bible studies, take Communion, you listen confidentially to the hurts and complaints of the people. All the time you have worked to promote the overall health of the church and to make the pastor appear better than he really is.

I can never thank you enough for all that you have done. I have learned much from you and your style of leadership and your acceptance of all people. It has been such a joy to see your heart soften over the years from when you first arrived. I attribute much of the success for turning around Central to you. Your foyer and prayer ministry has worked miracles. Most have no idea how much you do. When I read your weekly report of work you did, I feel tired and lazy. God has blessed you with incredible energy and passion. I love it when you smile and say, "Pastor, I just love my job!" I believe you. My prayer is that when you are down or discouraged for whatever reason you will continue to find your strength and hope in the Lord Jesus Christ. I pray that you will continue to receive a fresh anointing every day and you live each moment in the power of the Holy Spirit.

Marcia, I am proud to call you my Associate Pastor and honored to work with and for you. Let us pray that God gives us many more years of fruitful labor for Him in His vineyard. Only He knows the future. But I am confident of one thing; God is good all the time and all the time God is good![13]

God bless you Marcia! I love you from the bottom of my heart. Central loves you! ~Your Humble Servant,

Pastor Mike

As I read this letter, tears fell from my eyes because I realized that Pastor Mike deeply appreciated my service, that he was more aware of my tasks than I realized, and that he was human—but not just an ordinary man. It takes a real leader to be as observant, transparent (perhaps a bit vulnerable), and expressive as he was in this letter.

I have often wished that Pastor Mike did not mention my ill health and my fixed income, but I have forgiven him. Seriously, I consider myself just as healthy as any wo/man, especially after I have done my best and God does the rest. I also maintain that I have been richer than the wealthiest wo/man alive. Why? Because of the biblical paradox, "Give, and it shall be given unto you; good measure, pressed down, and shaken together, and running over, shall men give into your bosom. For with the same measure that ye mete withal it shall be measured to you again."(Luke 6:38). This has been proven and received time and time again. My secrets to physical, financial, and spiritual success are returning my tithe, ungrudgingly giving an offering, cheerfully giving to the needy—but foremost—serving, trusting, and unapologetically obeying God.

Freely Received? ... Freely Give!

This chapter must not end without me saying how blessed I have been after giving (sometimes all that I have) to others. And how richly blessed others have been by me just soliciting funds on their behalf from the most caring people I have ever known.

- One particular week, I gave someone $200.00. It was all I had left to purchase some miscellaneous items after paying all my bills and making a deposit to my savings account. Well, someone needed just that amount. So, instead of spending it on me, I gave it all to the individual. Since I do not like withdrawing from savings, I just decided to go without my small incidentals that week. When I arrived at church that Sabbath, I laid my clipboard down, and "someone" (I never found out who) had placed $200 cash—inside my clipboard that I had left for a moment or two on the counter in the foyer—with no explanation. My intention was to find out who had done this? How did they know I was short this amount? And why won't someone admit to it? Then the Lord said, "Stop. I did it! Go in peace."
- One Sabbath morning, I headed out to church without sufficient gasoline in my vehicle. That particular week I was broke "as broke as a plate, " I used to say. Anyway, here I was at church hoping to get back home and push my way through the weekend until Monday when for sure there would be

monies in my account. Well, one of the leaders came up to me that morning (the late **Rick Ricketts**). He shook my hand then withdrew his, leaving $60.00 cash in my palm. Oops! I walked swiftly after him asking if he wanted me to put this money in a tithe envelope for him. He looked at me and said, "This is for you—a gift—for all you are doing for this church." I started to speak, and he simply walked away. I was so choked up that I could not even say, "Thank you!" But God knew my need and impressed it on his heart. Rick's widow, **Barbara**, follows this path as well. There is never a time that a financial need is brought to her from a family in need that she does not contribute.

Over the years, it gradually became my motto to find a way to help someone after listening to their desperately stated need. Many will never, or will seldom, accept any help. And when they say, "Just pray," then *just pray*. But after praying with them, I pray some more by myself and ask God what would He have me to do? Then I await His direction in trying to figure out a way to help alleviate their problem or refer them to someone who can. I believe that we do not always need to refer members of our flock to social services when we know of those within our congregation who can, and are willing to, help—especially financially—without the person in need having to go through an application process.

This brings me to three additional stories worth mentioning.

(1) Once there was a young mother, in desperate need of a vehicle. She had no support outside the church, and, based on her marginally *high* income, she was not able to receive food stamps from the government. Now, her car had broken down (as had happened many times before), and she needed $600.00 to put a down payment on a new vehicle so she and her children could have transportation. I got on my e-mail right away and sent memos to three or four individuals. One couple, upon arriving at the church, gave me an envelope with $600.00 in cash—Elder Ben and Betty Barton. It has been almost five years now since that mother purchased the new vehicle and, as

of this writing, she still has that car. When we are not able to give, we certainly can ask others to help.

(2) Another amazing response to an immediate need stated by someone on a Sabbath morning was for $300.00. I had just arrived at the church and did not know who to ask to help this young woman. I jokingly said to the first couple walking in, whom I had gotten to know quite well, that I was soliciting funds for someone who was very much in need. They both almost emptied their wallets. I said, "No, no. Don't give me all your cash!" And they reminded me that God had been good to them and there was more. Now, as I recount this story I do remember that two years before this same couple (Ron and Vicki) had contributed $1,000 to help another single mother who was leaving town with her young son to settle in another city and needed these funds as a security deposit for their new place. The recipient was shocked, and her tears of sorrow turned into tears of Joy. When she expressed her gratitude, the benefactors said that they had been where these beneficiaries were, and God had done similar things for them. And all they wanted to do now was give back.

(3) Finally, among the many, many individuals who have contributed to the needy is my friend, Roan Dunn. She is an RN and has been a member of Central Church for years—prior to my arriving. Roan is a medical professional with a very caring heart. Once she met a young, single mother who was financially strapped and needing help. She introduced her family to our church and also assisted in helping that mother get back on her feet. Roan chose not just to give financially but to guide this parent into financial recovery through educational opportunities. She was instrumental in registering this mother for a CNA (Certified Nursing Assistant) course, and then she volunteered to babysit with the kids while mom was in class. I thought this was beyond amazing! As it turned out, this mother passed the course and was able to move beyond just surviving to also earning, building on her education, and helping others as she too had been helped.

There are numerous stories such as these that happened during my tenure at Central Church, but I have chosen to share just a few. There are many who gave what they could and many who received and gave back in tangible ways. Many times, when we pray, our actions (not just our prayers) are indicative of our relationship with, and trust in, God. Not everyone in need is a beggar or a scam artist. God will give his servants discernment and direction. Do not be afraid to meet the challenges of the day. He is wisdom, joy, and peace.

Chapter 6

Listening to God

In John 10: 27, 28 Jesus is quoted as saying, "My sheep hear my voice, and I know them, and they follow me: And I give unto them eternal life; and they shall never perish, neither shall any man pluck them out of **my** hand." [emphasis added].

In this chapter I have chosen to share some spectacular events that have taken place in my life over many years—reassuring me that God hears and answers prayers, that He is in total control of my life, and that He wants me to always trust Him.

When Church Came to Me

Have you ever desperately wanted to go to church and for some reason it was not possible? Well, I was caught in that dilemma one Sabbath morning while away from my home state of Florida, my husband, our two sons, and our church family.

It was in the late 1980s, while working as a Liquidation Technician for the FDIC (Federal Deposit Insurance Corporation) that I was sent on a bank liquidation detail to the city of Chicago for three weeks (and two weekends). Since our team flew into Chicago's O'Hare Airport, which was very close to our hotel and to the financial institution to which we were assigned, there was no authorization given for car rentals. Therefore, we took a shuttle from the airport to the hotel, and the bank building was in walking distance of the hotel. So, no need to waste the taxpayers' money.

71

It was extremely windy and cold in Chicago, and, when the first weekend arrived, I so wished we could fly back to Florida. However, this was not the plan. So, when Sabbath morning arrived, I started to call the different Adventist Churches that were in the yellow pages. After calling three churches and receiving no answer, I almost gave up. But then, on the next call someone answered. I explained to the receptionist that I was new in town and wanted to attend church but had no transportation. After giving her my location, she responded that there was no one who could come to that area now, but if I could get a ride to the church, then after lunch someone would take me back to my hotel. That seemed like it would work, but I knew of no one who could transport me to her church. So, I aborted the idea. Now, what would I do locked in a hotel room all day and missing out on congregational worship? Ah, no problem. I thought to myself, *Lord, I will just go down to the restaurant and see if there is* someone there who needs a word from You and share that with them. This sounded like a good plan to me, and perhaps this was what God wanted me to do. So, I got dressed in *church clothes* (no hat or gloves, of course) and followed my plan.

> *Have you ever desperately wanted to go to church and for some reason it was not possible? When I could not be in church, God brought church to me. He does and always will grant the desires of our heart when our desires are toward Him.*

Upon exiting the elevator to the ground level and lobby of the building, I saw numerous nicely dressed individuals walking through the doors and heading to one of the ballrooms. I walked up to the desk and asked one of the hotel attendants what was happening here today. And he asked me, "Have you ever heard of Ben Carson?" I responded, "If he is the surgeon who recently operated on the Binder twins who were joined at the head, then who hasn't heard of him?" The young man continued, "Well, Dr. Carson is lecturing here today, and that is why the hall is filling up. Would you like to go hear him?" *Why not, I thought, since I am unable to attend a church in the city, this would be the next best thing.* I then said to the attendant, "Why not! But I do not have a ticket." He responded, "Follow me!" This employee, passing all those who were already seated, ushered me to the front of the auditorium. I thanked him, but chose, however, not to sit in the front row. I settled instead for a seat at the end of the second row, as some attendees might have thought I was someone special...but I was—a child of God.

As I sat in my chair, I was beyond astonished and could hardly cease to smile as I felt so loved by God. Of course, I thought this would be a medical lecture, and I was prepared for some boredom and perhaps a speedy exit. The event began with music. And the audience was encouraged to sing songs that we would only hear in church. At this writing, approximately 32 years later, I do not remember the songs we sang, but what I felt was that God knew my desire to worship and praise Him and He had planned this gathering just for me. I do not remember what Dr. Carson spoke about, whether he talked about his book or the surgery, but I felt the Spirit of the Lord in my soul, and, even though I was told by the attendant that I could go up after the lecture and talk to the surgeon, I was not thinking about doing that. When the session was over, I raced to my hotel room, fell on my knees, and thanked God for bringing church to me. I was more interested in the Creator and His love for me than this renowned doctor whom God had used to satisfy my quest. I will never forget that, when I could not be in church, God brought church to me. He does and always will grant the desires of our heart when our desires are toward Him.

In Nassau, Bahamas

Here is another astounding answer to prayer to which many can probably relate. In the early days, when my consultants and I began traveling with The Complete Woman/Man Seminars, we made a commitment to God that, wherever He sent us, we would go—whether or not those requesting the seminar could afford to pay the fee. It is a promise we have always kept.

Well, in 1995 while living in Atlanta, Georgia, we received a request to facilitate a weekend of workshops for individuals in Nassau who were "Living Single." The coordinator of this event stated that we had been highly recommended by one of their singles who had attended our workshop in Kissimmee, Florida.

After sending her our financial (discounted) quote for church organizations, the coordinator responded that they just could not afford us. So, because of our promise never to say no to anyone, I told her that we would look into the matter and see if there could be a compromise. After praying, God led me to see that here was a chance to travel to a place I had never been, to help people who needed our services, and to enjoy some time on the beautiful beach outside the hotel.

In our negotiating, I was able to joyfully say to the coordinator that I would be traveling alone to present the weekend seminars and would forego the gratuity of $1,000. I only needed them to cover charges for my round-trip air fare, hotel accommodations and meals. This would be both work and indeed a vacation for me. All was well, and both sides were happy.

Upon arrival at the airport in Nassau, I was greeted by our hostess, a beautiful woman of God. On our way to the hotel, she gave me an envelope with $1,000 cash! She told me of how the singles in her church, in eager anticipation of this event, worked together in preparing and selling meals, so these funds could be available. After saying to my hostess, "Thank you so very much!" I then smiled (an inward smile to myself), and God understood it as a "Thank you, Lord!" And He responded, *I will always take care of you*!

At a Branson, Missouri, Resort

Betty Anderson and I were the two consultants serving as facilitators for a Women's Ministry Weekend at a popular resort in Branson, Missouri. Even though this was being sponsored on a conference-wide level, the regional conference Women's Ministry coordinator committed only to pay for our travel costs, registration fees, and meals. We would be responsible for the costs of our hotel rooms and there would be no gratuity—only an opportunity for us to sell my book.

No problem! Betty and I would then share a room and our corporation would absorb the hotel costs. We believed this would be a great opportunity to share, enjoy, and be blessed. Betty and I had not seen each other in months, and this was also an opportunity for us to get away from Florida and Colorado to enjoy some "sister" time and meet new people. The resort was amazingly beautiful, and the program participants and other presenters were great! It was worth it. However, two nights in a hotel was an astronomical cost for us. But, we had committed, we had prayed, and we believed God that He would provide.

I had been asked to be the first speaker at the start of the conference on Friday evening. As I sat, waiting to present to these women who appeared eager to launch into this wonderful weekend of blessings for them and us, my heart was heavy, and I could not quite explain why. After a brief introduction by our host, and, before it was my turn to speak, one of the attendees sang a song. The title of the rendition was: "He'll Do It Again for You."[14] Wow! The woman who sang was fantastic! The words and the music seemed to put life into my body, and I could not wait to leap (as it were) to the lectern for one of the best presentations God had ever allowed me to give. Betty, too, was immensely powerful when she presented in the afternoon of the next day. It seemed the Spirit of God outshone Himself in her presentation. And here, once again, we were all so spiritually nourished. At the end of the conference, we were still very apprehensive about the financial situation we would put our corporation in because of our compensatory negotiations.

Well, here is how God's financial provision came— allowing us to leave not *in the red*, but *in the black* at the end of the conference. Almost two weeks before this engagement, it was confirmed that our publisher, TEACH Services, had drop-shipped two boxes of my book, *The Complete Wo/Man*,[15] to the hotel. These we would display for sale and signing on Saturday night as we would be checking out of the hotel early Sunday morning.

It happened that, when we arrived at the hotel on Friday afternoon and requested to see where the books were stored and affirmed when they would be needed, the hotel staff could not find the boxes. We had written proof that they were delivered, but they were nowhere to be found. The staff continued to search, and we continued to pray. On Saturday afternoon, the books were still missing. Well, there we were no books, and that meant no opportunity to get them into the hands of the women that night. We were so disappointed. Well, low and behold, before the conference displays were to take place, the hotel found my books! And thank God, we then sold all of them! Of course, monies from the sale of these books were not for profit. We had to pay our publisher for the reprints and the shipment. There was still the cost of two nights in the hotel that we had placed on our credit card, and the concern of figuring out how our corporation would be compensated.

God came through again. On Sunday morning when I picked up the check-out notice that was slipped under our door, the total for our two nights' hotel stay was, "No charge!"

The Hosiery Story

God has a way of showing us what happens when we do not listen and what can happen when we do. This is an intimate, humorous, and incisive story of not listening to God and how He allows us to follow in our own footsteps but yet arrive at the place where He intended for us to be all along.

One of the local churches I had formerly attended (I will not say which) was having a Women's Weekend. I had just settled into the neighborhood and was new to the church and its people. Nevertheless, the leaders were aware that I had a seminar ministry. Though I was not overly bodacious, and they had never heard me give a presentation, it was still disconcerting to me that I was not asked to contribute to any phase of the Women's Weekend program.

The guest speaker for the event was a prominent and beautiful lady whom I had not had the privilege of meeting, so I looked forward to attending and receiving the blessing God had in store for all of us. That Friday before the program, I went shopping at my favorite store. An inner voice kept saying, "Purchase a new pair of hosiery." This was repeated three times. I did not ignore the voice, but I argued that I had a pair at home (with a small run); personal funds were low; and, since I would not be actively involved in anything tomorrow, I would wear what I had and no one would notice the tear. I was wrong, of course, and should have listened to God.

The next morning, I got nicely dressed and hoped that the run in my nylons would not extend any further than where it currently stopped. However, I took extra precautions and applied clear nail polish to the edge of the tear, rushed off to Sabbath School, and took my seat. Near the end of our study and about a half-hour before the main service was to begin, one of the ladies came to me and whispered, "Marcia, are you able to preach for us today? Our guest speaker has laryngitis and cannot present the sermon." My response was that I would have to rush home and get notes from one of the presentations I had previously done. Thank Heaven I resided only 15 minutes at most from the church. So, I rushed home and gathered my materials. As I drove back to the building, the only thing I could think of was, *I should have purchased the new pair of hosiery; please forgive me, Lord*!

I was new, uninvited to speak, and basically unknown to this church, but it was God's intention for me to speak that day. What I learned was this: (1) always obey when you *hear* the voice of The Good Shepherd, even when you do not understand His commands, (2) always be prepared to represent Him, and (3) if the experience does not humble you, then there is a problem. Even though I knew God had done this—in the back of my mind as I spoke—I kept wondering if the platform of ladies sitting behind me were looking at my hosiery run or were they listening to the message? I continue to learn always to listen to God. That day I was reprimanded, forgiven, and humbled by Him. I will never forget that experience!

On 3ABN and Mad at God

By 2011, even though we (our consultants and I) had been inter-
viewed on at least three television programs in the 1990's with The
Complete Woman/Man Seminars—and those included the *Good
Day* morning show with host Rebecca Randall in Orlando, Florida;
Babbie's House with Babbie Mason in Atlanta, Georgia; and the
Pastor Keith Ellis program also in Atlanta—I wanted us to be on
other networks. Since I liked watching *The View* live from New
York and wanted to meet Barbara Walters and Whoopi Goldberg
someday, I dreamed of that and asked God if that show would
be a good place for us, and, if so, I prayed, "Dear Lord, please
make this happen!" Well, pray on because God hears, and He will
answer—but not always in the way we think.

It was during the latter part of 2010 that I met, via telephone,
Cheri Peters, host of "Celebrating Life in Recovery" that airs on
3ABN (Three Angels Broadcasting Network). Cheri had called the
Central Church office needing some information and I returned
her call. We talked at length, and she asked about my ministry
and my passion. At the end of our talk, she said: "I will remember you, Marcia, and have you
on the show in the future." Well,
"Okay," I said but was not sure
I would hear from her again.
Cheri's program was extremely
popular, and I had watched several episodes, but I really did
not want to be on that program
to talk about any insecurities or
recoveries. I wanted to be on ABC and, if not, then "3ABN Today"
to talk about our ministry and forthcoming events. Anyway, if this
was God's answer, I would watch and wait to see the fulfillment.

> *Even though we
> did not get to share
> what we wanted to
> communicate, God
> knew what His people
> needed to hear.*

One morning (about three months later) right after getting
up from my knees, I received a call from a producer at 3ABN,
requesting my presence for an interview with them in West
Frankfort, Illinois. I thought, *Lord, you have answered my prayer,
but this is not the network I asked you for.* What is going on? Well,

of course, I said, "Yes," to the producer. Verbal and written communication followed. A copy of my first two books were sent to them for added information. A date was set, and plans were made for recording. In March 2011, one of my consultants and I arrived at the studio for the interview. It was our first time on the 3ABN campus. It was a lovely place to be and to see. We were greeted warmly and accommodated extremely well.

So, why was I mad at God you ask. Well here is the story. I thought we were going to be interviewed on "3ABN Today" where the stories would be about our ministry, vision, and future projects. As it turned out, however, upon arriving at the studio, we were told that after reading my books, it was decided that the recording would be with Cheri on the "Celebrating Life in Recovery" program. And, instead of speaking about our ministry, the program would be addressing the subject of "Rebellion." Wow! Now my entire mindset was changed. I did not think I was a rebel and had not taken the time to focus on rebellion until now. Well, we asked for ten extra minutes in the green room where a lot of discussion went on between myself and my consultant. She was a bit upset, and I spent some time calming her down. I was mad at God and at the network because I did not want to discuss this subject during a recording session.

As it was, God (and 3ABN) had the final word. I switched hats after five minutes and said, "Lord, Your will be done!" Again, I had to repent because I knew this was God's working. The interview, "The Rebel" went very well and we departed, thanking God that Cheri kept her word, for the opportunity to appear on her program. After the recording, we were told that the program would be aired within a few months, and it was. Even though we did not share any contact information at that recording, my first knowledge that the program had been broadcast came from two women from overseas and a girlfriend living in Michigan. They expressed how much they were blessed by hearing the testimonies on rebellion. I was not surprised to hear their responses, as I knew this program was totally about what Our Creator wanted and not about us. Even though we did not get to share what *we* wanted to communicate, God knew what *His people* needed to hear.

A Prayer for Reconciliation

While living in Colorado Springs, I have had the privilege of meeting numerous people and becoming professional friends with many, just an acquaintance with some, and good friends with a few individuals—especially ladies around my age. For the past few years, my friend (whom I will call Audrey) has become one of my two personal, Catholic friends—both of whom are very committed to their faith and very faithful in their loyalty to family, profession, and friends.

One day while leaving the gym, I had an urgent phone call from Audrey. She wanted to know if I would come by her house and pray with her for their two adult children. We had never prayed together before, neither had we ever discussed any family problems. So, before responding, I placed her on hold as I transitioned into my car with the cell phone. Then, three quick thoughts flashed through my mind: (1) She prays with rosaries; I do not; (2) Lord, I'm awfully sweaty right now, and I should go home first; and (3) I don't even have my Bible from which to read some consoling thoughts and don't I need that? Then, just as fast, the answer came from God, *Go just as you are, and I am with you.* I immediately obeyed and told Audrey I would be there shortly. As I drove past my street and hit the highway, my prayer was that God would use me in a way that He has never done before, and He did.

It was two weeks before Easter, and it appeared that for years Audrey's children had not spoken to each other. Consequently, there were several Easter celebrations where children, and grandchildren, did not celebrate together as had been their custom as a family. What should have been a joyous time, was an incredibly sad time for Audrey and her husband as they approached this special weekend. Audrey did not want to go through this experience another year. The story that echoed filled my heart with empathy, and nothing mattered then except to fall on our knees in prayer to our Savior. I spoke to God as my dearest friend, and I did not know what His answer would be, but I knew He had heard my prayer for this family and had honored our faith in Him.

Well, Easter came and went. About a week later, I was driving home from the gym and wondered what had happened with Audrey's family. Right then, my cell phone rang, and I heard the very melodious and excited voice of my friend. She said, "Marcia, we had the best Easter dinner and gathering we have ever experienced. Our children and grandchildren were together at our house. Thank you for praying for us." Wow!

While we did not know how God would answer, I knew that He would because I have learned to listen to Him and have been more than blessed when I have done as He instructs. I pray the same for all my family, friends, and acquaintances. I pray this too for all my enemies. Listen to God, obey His Word, and submit to His will.

Chapter 7

Mentors and Friends

I t is said that the three C's of mentorship and the roles for the mentor to play are "Consultant, Counselor, and Cheerleader." No one can be successful in life by standing alone. Successful people have been encouraged and mentored by something or someone. For sure, my success in ministry over the past decade at Central Church can be attributed not only to God, but also to Pastor Mike and Brenda Maldonado. Therefore, in this chapter you will read of just a few of the many experiences I have been blessed to share with this incredible duo who nurtured and included me in everything that was educational, uplifting, and profitable. And truly I have learned to be a servant-leader from their example.

Volunteer Appreciation Brunch

The Maldonado's first expression of love sparkled very brightly when (during my first year at Central Church) it was announced that they would be hosting a Volunteer Appreciation Brunch for all volunteers at the designated time and place, which was to be on a beautiful Sunday morning at a garden venue in Colorado Springs. When we arrived, there was a huge, white tent, under which round tables and chairs were magnificently arranged, with all the accoutrements that one can imagine at an outdoor gala engineered by people of class. The cooks and servers were none other than our pastor, his wife and two of their friends. I must admit that this was a first for me: my first year at Central, my first time really getting to know these people, and my first time feeling so collectively honored and blown away.

We, the volunteers, were taken aback by this token of love and, when we learned that this was an event they wanted to do annually, we turned the tables on them. We decided to honor *them* yearly, which they vehemently opposed, but the majority ruled, and we stepped up our game by honoring them every October in keeping with Pastors Appreciation month. The membership felt so good about this decision (since this was perhaps the only church activity we had complete control over.)

The Maldonado's have been equally blessed by our expressions of love and appreciation as well, but they really regret not being able to exercise their option of doing the same again for us.

Marcia, You Are Invited

After becoming Assistant for Pastoral Care, it held true to form that Pastor Mike or Brenda would always invite me to attend community events with them, and Pastor would always introduce me as his associate. He even placed my name on his business cards. That was an honor, but many of the events to which I was invited were for pastors and their wives and I felt a bit awkward in attending, but once arriving at the conference or gathering, and getting settled in, I was always glad I had accepted their invitation. Not only did we attend local events together, but also out-of-town conferences. Even though there have been many such occasions, here I have chosen to share only three.

1. In 2017, we attended a Focus on the Family Pastors Appreciation Luncheon that was very memorable. Before entering the dining area, we met numerous Colorado Springs vendors from different specialties who shared information with attendees. This was very educational for me and many others. The luncheon ambiance was fabulous, and guests could tell that a lot of thought had gone into planning. This was perhaps the first

time I was able to observe Pastor Mike and Brenda sit and enjoy themselves without interruption. No hassles, no disturbances, and no obvious worries. I was impressed as I observed how attentively they were listening to the guest speaker—especially when they were both such excellent speakers themselves. When I finally stopped taking pictures, I quieted down to enjoy the program and the company of four other new acquaintances—and one of our members—who were also at our table. While driving home, all I could think was, *How cool was that!*

2.	In June 2018, we were invited to attend Clergy Day at Peterson Air Force Base. The invitation was extended to pastors and chaplains to partner with Peterson Chapel at a one-day meeting on their campus. Of course, Pastor extended the invitation for me to attend as well. This was a wonderful opportunity to meet local clergy—men and women—from other faiths. We spent several hours on the base, dining, listening to presentations, touring the facility, and learning about the needs of military families. Attendees were presented with ways in which the faith community in Colorado Springs could be of support spiritually and emotionally to military men and women and their families. Had I not been so extremely busy, I would have made a commitment to meet some of the needs, but any added responsibility at that time would have been too much for me to effectively handle. This event, however, was another great exposure to the sundry needs within our municipal area of service.

3.	The third of all the invites we enjoyed together I have left for last because of its length and because it was a good (and perhaps not-so-good) experience. It took place at a 2017 Mid-America Union Conference Pastors Convention held in Omaha, Nebraska. Pastors, chaplains, their wives, and families were invited. Pastor Mike felt this would be a good experience for me and asked if I would be willing to attend. He suggested it would be terrific for me to meet some of the other conference leaders, pastors, and staff. Of course, here was another gift and a brief vacation for me. To avoid my paying of any travel costs, Pastor Mike asked the church to pay for my plane ticket and categorically stated that he and Brenda would drive so I could fly. I was floored! "No. No," I said, but they insisted that they would drive [eight hours] so I would not experience any discomfort or expense on this trip. This was unbelievable. I could hardly contain myself just thinking how incredible this gesture was. And even at this writing I continue to stand amazed.

Because of my late registration and hotel availability, my hotel reservation was not in the Embassy Suites where the meetings took place and where the majority of attendees and presenters were housed. No problem. I was a guest at a hotel about five blocks away and in walking distance. The Maldonado family and I stayed in touch by phone. We had all arrived safely. That evening, after check-in, I navigated my way to the meeting center at the Embassy Suites—a nice, somewhat quiet walk to their location. After the opening session and worship was over, Pastor Mike and Brenda said they would walk me to my hotel, as it had gotten dark. I stated that I would be okay since my hotel was only five blocks away, but they insisted. Every night after that, this was their task— except for the last night. But before getting to that last night, I will share some in-between moments that will stay with me for as long as I live—some really great moments and just one that was not so fantastic. Among the highlights were these: (1) observing how well-planned the event was, (2) seeing pastors and their families enjoying their time together, (3) observing how relaxed and happy Pastor Mike and Brenda were, and (4) observing the many people who were just so glad to see or meet each other. Not only that, but Pastor Mike would always introduce me as his associate. I kept asking him not to say that, but to no avail. So, I began to stay out of their perimeter whenever possible as they mingled with other guests. This conference had now become one of the best gatherings I had ever attended. Until ...

One day, the Rocky Mountain Conference (RMC) leaders rented/reserved the upper floor of a nearby restaurant for a special luncheon for pastors and their wives. While walking toward the venue, I was introduced to two long-time friends of Pastor Mike and Brenda: Pastor Tom and Gingerlei Fuiono Tupito. They became friends during their school days at Andrews University. We all sat together at our table, and, as the two couples were catching up on old times, I was thinking how cool this was. During the course of our dining together, "Ginger" and I were getting to know each other. Near the end of our meal, it was announced that after lunch there would be a table of gifts for all the "ladies" and each should take a giftbag before leaving the building. Well, as Ginger and I walked toward the table, she took her bag, and I reached to get one myself. As I reached to procure a package, one of the leader's wives standing at her post and over-looking the gifts, grabbed the bag from my hand and said, "This is for pastor's wives only." If I could have been embarrassed, I certainly would have been. However, I just said, "Oh!" and moved on. As I did, I thought, *Well, I am technically not a pastor's wife, and I am the only one here who isn't, but what is one bag of books? Oh well.* I have been discriminated against so many times in my life in America, but this was quite an *ouch* coming from this group, this woman— this Christian. As I smiled and exited with Ginger, I could see the pain in her eyes for me and the questioning look on her face. She then said to me, "Marcia, you can have my bag." But no. I could and would not take hers. There would have been no significance and no satisfaction for me in taking her gift (which I really did not need).

Inasmuch as I will never forget that incident, I will never forget Ginger and the love she showed that day. (We became friends at that conference, not because of the occurrence, but because she was a woman to love. I saw my friend twice after our meeting, and she died within two years after that.) While I will never forget the *ouch*, I, too, will never forget Ginger.

On the last evening before we left Omaha, I knew Pastor Mike and Brenda had wanted to walk me to my hotel as they had done the two previous nights. I could not let them. When I saw how their colleagues were eagerly embracing them, while others were waiting in line to just say, "Hello," the Holy Spirit said to me, *Let them have their night; go home; I'm walking with you,* and I obeyed.

By the time I had gotten to my hotel and was getting ready for bed, Brenda called to find out where I was and stated that they had been looking all over for me. I reiterated what the Holy Spirit had told me and assured them I was simply fine. They were not happy with me, but I am glad their friends, who so eagerly wanted to spend a little time with them, had gotten their wish. Pastor Mike and Brenda have always gone out of their way to make me feel accepted, loved, and valuable, and I will always remember that about them. They are a couple with the highest caliber of competence, hospitality, and correctness. I love them with all my heart for their expressed appreciation and mentorship.

In pastoral care ministry, Pastor Mike has been my boss, my mentor, and my friend. Our ethnicity has never been a factor in our work together because we see humanity as one. So, the fact that he had been born in Mexico and I was a Jamaican was irrelevant in the ministry God had for us. We were both committed in purpose and that was the only prerequisite for being a member of the pastoral team.

Perhaps the most amazing part of our relationship was that of our approach to ministry. Three examples of our major differences are as follows: (1) our Bible preference. Pastor Mike likes the NIV (New International Version) and I much prefer the KJV (King James Version); (2) Pastor Mike will go to the *lowest valley* and climb the *highest mountain* to find lost or missing souls and encourage them back to the church no matter how long it takes, and my opinion usually is, "Pastor, they know where the church is located, and God will draw them back if they are willing to be guided. Let us stay busy working with the flock that is present." And (3) Pastor Mike likes more contemporary musical anthems, and I am content singing hymns. Because of these differences, I have jokingly said, "Pastor and I go to the same church, but we are not of the same mind."

Though Pastor Mike and I differed in certain aspects of methodology and appeal, we were parallel in organizational management and protocols. So, here are three similarities into which I grew as he mentored me: (1) Pastor believed in arriving at an engagement (at the church or elsewhere) on time. Consequently,

whenever there was a service, a meeting, or a Bible class scheduled, I would make sure to be there at least a half hour to an hour
early; (2) Pastor Mike liked that I could sense what was required
to fulfill the task without a spoken request. I loved having that
inherent sense as well, and (3) all of us leaders grew into having a
keen observance of when things were out of place (e.g., "trash" on
the floor, in the walkways, or on the pews). Anything that did not
belong or would show disrespect to or desecrate the house of God
had to be removed.

It seemed I was misled into thinking that I was meticulous
and appearance conscious—until I met this man. This does not
mean we were vain or overly concerned about how we or others
appeared. On the contrary, there was never a concern about how
a worshipper dressed. Our directive was to welcome all who came
into the house of God. It was remarkably interesting to know that
someone once called our pastor to say he wanted to attend church,
but only had a pair of jeans to wear and asked if that was okay.
Well, not only was it okay, but Pastor Mike and all the male elders
wore jeans the next Sabbath so this worshipper would not feel he
was out of place. (I am still wondering why I was not consulted and
asked to wear jeans myself; but I am glad they made the transformation and did not ask Marcia.) Pastor Mike was more concerned
about visitors' perceptions of the house of God when they walked
into the building or connected with our website, bulletins, news-
letters, etc. Everything had to be correctly represented. Pastor
Mike is bilingual (Spanish and English) but his grammar was, and
is, perfect in both languages. This was a blessing for me and a
great similarity. I actually thought I was a perfectionist until I met
Pastor Mike. But his perfectionism topped the chart. Our friend,
Kari Uusinarkaus, MD, jokingly says this disposition is a "condition" for which there is no medication. And, by the way, our dear
doctor Kari suffers from this condition as well.

There was never a task that Pastor Mike would assign to which
I did not say, "Yes," and embrace with confidence and ability. And
there was never any inquiry or need that came into the office via
telephone that I would not appropriately address. However, I
remember one evening, while winding down my work at the office,

I received a phone call from a mother who lived out of state and was concerned about her daughter in a nearby city of Colorado Springs. I listened to the story about her daughter—an incredibly sad and unfortunate situation—and I offered to help. After terminating the call, however, I realized that I should not have consented to intervene in such a fiasco as this was truly out of my realm. I should have recommended another resource. *How could I have said yes?* I thought. I felt dreadful and knew that my "yes" should have been a "no." My heart was heavy because I wanted to help but knew I should not. So, I thought, *How do I get out of this? Dear Lord, please help me! I do not want to renege on my promise, but this is too great a responsibility for me.*

By then, everyone had left the office, and I started to leave. While going across the church's parking lot, I noticed Pastor Mike's car was parked on the other side of the church building. *What is he doing here*, I thought. *Well, let me go in and see.* As I entered the fellowship hall, there was our pastor in the kitchen. When I asked, "For whom are you preparing a meal, Pastor?" He replied, "The children's choir is rehearsing this evening, and this is for them after rehearsal." Wow! I was so grateful that God had him there and that he was willing to listen to my problem. I had wanted to be a blessing, but this was way over my head. After explaining the situation to my mentor, he responded in a way that I did not think he would. Pastor Mike quoted a Scripture, and then he said,

"Marcia, not everyone who is lost wants to be found and not everyone who has chosen to deliberately cut ties with family members wants to be reconciled. We must understand and respect that. I am glad you feel this is not a task for you and that you recognize your limitations. Call it a day and be at peace!"

> *Not everyone who is lost wants to be found and not everyone who has chosen to deliberately cut ties with family members wants to be reconciled. We must understand and respect that.*

I was so relieved that evening. The guilt of not being able to help as I had promised was lifted, and I felt free to recant. I rushed to my car after speaking with the pastor to call this dear mother and extend my regret that I would not be able to follow through as promised, and she understood. We prayed together and trusted God that He would bring forth the healing needed within her family and that the estrangement would end. Instead of feeling like a failure (as I would have felt without counsel), the mood which came over me was one of triumph and God's reminder that I am not a panacea—not a solution for every difficulty—just a willing and obedient servant.

I will close now with a brief story of my meeting a lady in the grocery store, and we began to talk. After our initial greeting, this lady asked if I was a Christian and stated she had not been to church in a long time. Of course, I invited her to attend Central Church. Her first question then was, "What type of a person is your pastor?" I had a list of things I wanted to say, but we were both in a hurry, and the Holy Spirit said, *Just say this*: "He reminds me of Jesus." Later, when I questioned the response I had been given, the Holy Spirit's explanation was, *Because Pastor Mike cloaks his brilliance in humility.*

Truly, it has been a blessing from God for me to have been allowed into the work and service of His church and to have been associated with Pastor Mike Maldonado and his family. I will forever treasure the privilege of knowing them and the experience, warmth, and godliness of a diverse, intergenerational, and loving church such as Colorado Springs Central. It has been an honor to serve as a servant-leader along with so many others!

Chapter 8

Hard to Walk Away

In December 2019, I was diagnosed with PAC (premature atrial contractions) after seeking medical attention for some symptoms that had recently manifested themselves. One of the suggested cures was to lower my stress level. Thus, I made a decision to retire as Pastoral Assistant at Central Church. My request was accepted, and I was awarded a beautiful plaque in December 2019, and then in January 2020, given a retirement dinner that was second to none. At my first retirement in 2010 from the Fourth Judicial in Colorado Springs, I was honored by my coworkers, supervisor, judges, and several attorneys and mediators, as I walked away from a cumulative 44 years of secular employment. Even though I knew I would miss my work experience with them, I was happy to be away from the rigors of the court and the "nine-to-five" obligations. However, leaving a servant-leadership position at Central Church, a position in which the Lord had placed me in, was extremely emotional!

I struggled with being away from all that I had loved for ten years, but I knew (from a dream) that my tenure at Central Church was over. So difficult was this ministerial exit that I began to feel as I had felt twenty-six years prior, after my husband's death. Not the emotions of sorrow or grief, but ambiguity as to what to concentrate on or do next. Should it be physical healing? Yes! Taking better care of myself? Sure! Writing another book? Why not! But I did not know where I belonged. Attending church and sitting in the pew just as I had so many years before God called me to volunteer—felt strange. It took six months for me to somewhat get adjusted to now living my life in a different manner. The only thing I was not dubious about was that God was holding me firmly. What was beyond this repositioning was unclear to me, but I figured God would reveal His plan for my life, or death, in His own appointed time. During those six months of my readjustment, I kept remembering a pastor friend of ours who had retired from the ministry and would visit our home from time to time when my family lived in Michigan. On one occasion I asked this pastor if he missed pastoring and what did he miss the most. His response was, "The phone doesn't ring anymore." He missed talking with

> *When I surrendered my life to God and the joy began, His presence with me (always, now, and forever) has been the true epilogue of a mortal life leading to the beginning of someday enjoying immortality and living with Christ throughout eternity.*

his members and felt a bit isolated. However, if someone had asked me this question after retiring from my duties at Central Church, the phone not ringing would not have been something I missed. It is not that I missed the people, as I still saw them, and felt connected, but not in the same way. Inwardly, there was just an awkwardness as to where I belonged, and what God had in store for me. My temporary introversion was not about my not wanting to mingle with people, but I believed this was exactly where God wanted me to be. So, I am praising Him and awaiting the next order of business. So, whether you are reading this book posthumously or while I am still here, know that our Father had this in mind for you and me.

Yes. It has been hard to walk away: painful, lonely at times, but very gratifying. As I reflect on my life there are many regrets. But,

when I surrendered my life to God and the joy began, His presence
with me (always, now, and forever) has been the true epilogue of
a mortal life leading to the beginning of someday enjoying immor-
tality and living with Christ throughout eternity.

Chapter 9

What's Next

Should I be blessed to live a few more years, there are some things I would still like to continue doing, such as telling others about Jesus, continuing my workouts at the gym, attending church, teaching Bible classes, keeping up with my friends via telephone and/or Facebook, continuing to care for my body by eating a low-carbohydrate/vegetable-protein diet, and allowing medical professionals to assist with my health care—as needed.

My greatest aspirations include having The Complete Woman/Man website rebuilt, posting seminars that were done when we first started with The Complete Woman/Man Seminars, and accepting invitations to do local and long-distance lectures—primarily to those who are fifty-five plus. Actually, before my PAC diagnosis, I had started on this path but was only able to do two such seminars before the COVID-19 pandemic came on scene. Nevertheless, if God should choose to heal our land, I would certainly be on the road again to do these talks, which I have entitled, "The Joy of Aging."

At my last lecture, which was local and only an hour's drive from my residence, I called a friend who was also traveling on another highway when he received my call. He was with another doctor (whom I also knew), and we all were speaking together on Bluetooth. I mentioned I was on my way to a Silver Ladies luncheon and that the subject of my talk was "The Joy of Aging."

One said, "Well that presentation shouldn't take more than three to four minutes!" I started laughing hysterically, while reprimanding him for making that statement. But, wouldn't you know it that, when I told this story as an icebreaker to my audience that day, they laughed uncontrollably as well. After the presentation, one of the ladies remarked that it was so good to hear a lecture from someone who could relate not only to the joys, but also to the challenges of aging. That meant a lot to me, and her statement increased my delight in wanting to pursue this course of public service to seniors and the elderly.

I have written this manuscript after seven decades of living. The last two decades I have spent in Our Master's service. There is no greater joy than working for God, devoting all energy to the cause of Christ, and reaping the blessings He bestows when we obey His Word and His voice. My most important expectation is being able to see Jesus when He returns at the end of this world— to raise the righteous from their graves to be caught up with those who are living at the time of His appearing to spend an eternity with our Savior in a place where sin will never reign again, according to 1 Thessalonians 4:13–17. I hope this will be your desire as well. Together, we will each sing, "This my song through endless ages, Jesus led me all the way."[16]

Chapter 10

Things I Have Learned

- You do not have to know someone to be courteous to them.
- Keenly observing one's actions will allow for the exercise of caution.
- Judging someone by appearance can be misleading; spending time with them can be revealing.
- Someone's definition of you is always wrong.
- What you think of yourself is usually right, as long as your thoughts are aligned with God's.
- God's definition of you is no less than accurate.
- Remember not to ask the elderly: "Remember when...."
- Both men and women are essential and needed in productive church leadership.
- One cannot move forward while looking back, but reflecting on good memories can move you to greater heights.
- As long as there is pretense in the heart, there will be hypocrites in the church.
- Jesus died for ALL people. Not for some or a few.
- I am no better than the wo/man who thinks s/he is better than me.
- Discovering and enhancing the good in a person places one way above the fray.
- If you think it is shameful to be humble, think again.

- If you want to stay married and happy, switch from being a private eye and become a self-searching, surrendered prayer warrior.
- It is disingenuous to remind someone of what you have done for them, and outrageous to try and remind God of what you have done for Him.
- God's forgiveness is a promise, not a maybe.

Bibliography

1. Armstead, Marcia B. *The Complete Wo/Man: An Index to the Heart*. Ft. Oglethorpe, GA: TEACH Services, Inc., 2002.
2. Armstead, Marcia B. *Fragrance of God's Love: An Autobiography through the Love of My Friends*. Ft. Oglethorpe, GA: TEACH Services, Inc., 2010.
3. Batterson, Mark. *The Circle Maker: Praying Circles around Your Biggest Dreams and Greatest Fears*. Grand Rapids, MI: Zondervan, 2016.
4. Armstead, Marcia B. *Fragrance of God's Love: An Autobiography through the Love of My Friends*. Ft. Oglethorpe, GA: TEACH Services, Inc., 2010.
5. Armstead, Marcia B. *The Complete Wo/Man: An Index to the Heart*. Ft. Oglethorpe, GA: TEACH Services, Inc., 2002.
6. *The Seventh-day Adventist Hymnal*. Hagerstown, MD: Review and Herald Publishing Association, 1985, "When We All Get to Heaven," page 633.
7. Ibid., "Marching to Zion," page 422.
8. Armstead, Marcia B. *The Complete Wo/Man: An Index to the Heart*. Ft. Oglethorpe, GA: TEACH Services, Inc., 2002.
9. Armstead, Marcia B. *Fragrance of God's Love: An Autobiography through the Love of My Friends*. Ft. Oglethorpe, GA: TEACH Services, Inc., 2010.
10. Maldonado, Michael. "From Mono-ethnic to Multi-ethnic: One Church's Journey, *NewsNuggets*, Rocky Mountain Conference of Seventh-day Adventists, July 2020.
11. *The Seventh-day Adventist Hymnal*. Hagerstown, MD: Review and Herald Publishing Association, 1985, "Redeemed!" page 337.

12. Ibid., "There is a Fountain," page 336.
13. Moen, Don, and Overstreet, Paul. "God Is Good All the Time." Integrity's Hosanna! Music and Scarlet moon Music, Inc., 1995.
14. Ehi, Ada. "He'll Do It Again for You." Loveworld Records, 2017.
15. Armstead, Marcia B. *The Complete Wo/Man: An Index to the Heart*. Ft. Oglethorpe, GA: TEACH Services, Inc., 2002.
16. *The Seventh-day Adventist Hymnal*. Hagerstown, MD: Review and Herald Publishing Association, 1985, "All the Way," page 516.

TEACH Services, Inc.

P U B L I S H I N G

We invite you to view the complete
selection of titles we publish at:
www.TEACHServices.com

We encourage you to write us
with your thoughts about this,
or any other book we publish at:
info@TEACHServices.com

TEACH Services' titles may be purchased in
bulk quantities for educational, fund-raising,
business, or promotional use.
bulksales@TEACHServices.com

Finally, if you are interested in seeing
your own book in print, please contact us at:
publishing@TEACHServices.com

We are happy to review your manuscript at no charge.